The Ultimate Burger Cookbook

The Ultimate Burger Cookbook

100 Tasty Recipes

This edition published by Parragon Books Ltd in 2014
LOVE FOOD is an imprint of Parragon Books Ltd

Parragon Books Ltd
Chartist House
15-17 Trim Street
Bath BA1 1HA, UK
www.parragon.com/lovefood

ISBN 978-1-4723-7461-5
S39052

Printed in China

New Photography by Mike Cooper
New Food Styling by Lincoln Jefferson
New Recipes by Tara Duggan
Internal Design by Lexi L'Esteve
Project Managed by Kerry Starr

Notes for the Reader
This book uses both metric and imperial measurements. Follow the same units of measurement
throughout; do not mix metric and imperial. All spoon measurements are level: teaspoons are
assumed to be 5 ml, and tablespoons are assumed to be 15 ml. Unless otherwise stated, milk is
assumed to be full fat, eggs and individual vegetables are medium, and pepper is freshly ground
black pepper. Unless otherwise stated, all root vegetables should be peeled prior to using.

Garnishes, decorations and serving suggestions are all optional and not necessarily included in
the recipe ingredients or method. The times given are an approximate guide only. Preparation
times differ according to the techniques used by different people and the cooking times may
also vary from those given. Optional ingredients, variations or serving suggestions have not
been included in the time calculations.

Picture acknowledgements
Raw Burgers with Freshly Ground Pepper © Linda Lewis/Getty Images (page 9)
Ingredients for Burgers © Leigh Beisch/Getty Images (page 9)

CONTENTS

THE HISTORY OF THE BURGER

NOT SURPRISINGLY, MORE THAN ONE PERSON HAS TAKEN CREDIT FOR INVENTING THE BEEF BURGER. WHILE HUMANS HAVE BEEN EATING BEEF MINCE PATTIES FOR CENTURIES, THE TERM 'HAMBURGER STEAK' STARTED POPPING UP IN THE UNITED STATES IN THE 1800s, SUPPOSEDLY NAMED FOR THE GERMAN IMMIGRANTS WHO ORDERED THEM IN RESTAURANTS. BUT THE QUESTION OF WHO STARTED PUTTING THESE BEEF MINCE 'STEAKS' BETWEEN SLICES OF BREAD IS WHERE THE CONTROVERSY LIES.

IT MIGHT HAVE BEEN IN 1885, AT A COUNTY FAIR IN SEYMOUR, WISCONSIN, WHERE CHARLES NAGREEN SERVED BEEF BURGER STEAKS BETWEEN PIECES OF BREAD FOR EASE OF CARRYING. OR IT COULD HAVE BEEN IN 1892 AT ANOTHER COUNTY FAIR IN AKRON, OHIO, WHEN FRANK MENSCHES WAS SAID TO RUN OUT OF SAUSAGE AND DECIDED TO MINCE FRESH BEEF FOR SANDWICHES INSTEAD. THE THIRD THEORY IS THAT LOUIS LASSEN INVENTED THE BURGER IN HIS SMALL DINER IN NEW HAVEN, CONNECTICUT, AT AROUND THE SAME TIME.

BEEF BURGERS SPREAD IN POPULARITY IN THE FIRST HALF OF THE TWENTIETH CENTURY, PROLIFERATING IN CHAIN RESTAURANTS THROUGHOUT SOUTHERN CALIFORNIA, AND HAVE LONG SINCE BECOME A SYMBOL OF THE AMERICAN DIET. BUT THEY SEEM TO BE POPULAR EVERYWHERE, SUCH AS IN AUSTRALIA, WHERE PEOPLE LOVE TO TOP THEIR BURGERS WITH PICKLED BEETROOT, AND SOMETIMES EVEN WITH A FRIED EGG AND PINEAPPLE (SEE PAGE 126). IN KOREA, THE SPICY FERMENTED CABBAGE KNOWN AS KIMCHI GOES ON TOP OF BURGERS (SEE PAGE 140), AND IN JAPAN, BENTO BURGERS FEATURE BUNS MADE OF COMPRESSED RICE (SEE PAGE 138).

POULTRY, FISH AND VEGETARIAN VERSIONS OF THE CLASSIC BEEF BURGER ARE NOW THE NORM, AND EVEN FOUR-STAR CHEFS HAVE EMBRACED BURGERS, STUFFING THEM WITH FOIE GRAS AND TRUFFLES OR SIMPLY USING THE HIGHEST-GRADE MEATS AND SERVING THEM WITH HOME-MADE CONDIMENTS. THIS BASIC AMERICAN FOODSTUFF NOW HAS PERMUTATIONS, HIGH AND LOW, IN ALMOST EVERY CORNER OF THE GLOBE.

EQUIPMENT

True to its humble origins, the beef burger is a low-tech food requiring not much more than a sharp knife for slicing tomatoes and a frying pan, grill or barbecue. Here is the only equipment you'll really need.

· Mixing bowls

· Spatula for flipping burgers

· Knives for slicing tomatoes (serrated works well), lettuce and other condiments

· Whisk for making sauces such as mayonnaise

· Frying pan or griddle pan. Look for heavy-based pans, which have better heat transfer, to create a better sear on your burgers

· Grill pan and rack

· Gas or charcoal barbecue

· Meat mincer or food processor (optional) to make the freshly minced Steakhouse Burger (see page 92)

KA-POW!

HOW TO MAKE THE PERFECT BURGER PATTY

Burgers are incredibly easy to prepare, and the only really important step, beyond not overcooking them, is forming the patty. The main thing to avoid is overworking the meat, which can result in tough, rather than tender and juicy, burgers.

Fresh beef mince is the easiest to work with, because it's both dry enough and sticky enough to bind well. Turkey, chicken and pork mince can be much wetter than beef and therefore harder to shape, but adding some breadcrumbs can help alleviate that problem. Also, wetting your hands while forming the patties helps. The same applies to vegetarian burgers, which can be wet and difficult to shape.

To form patties, place the meat in a bowl, add all of the seasonings at once, then mix – preferably with your hands – just until the seasonings are fully integrated.

Divide the meat into portions, then gently form each portion into even-sized patties. If possible, make the patties slightly wider than the buns, because they will shrink during cooking. For the same reason, it also helps to make the edges of the patty thicker than the centre, or to add a dimple to the centre of the patty, so that when the meat contracts, the patty will end up evenly thick.

HOW TO COOK THE PERFECT BURGER

Quick cooking methods with high, dry heat are the best way to get burgers nicely browned on the outside while keeping them juicy inside.

Fried and Griddled
This is the classic diner method, which involves a hot frying pan and some cooking fat. The burgers cook over a medium-high heat until they develop a golden-brown crust.

Steamed
Steaming takes frying one step further to keep the meat extra-moist. While frying, just cover the burgers with a lid to finish cooking.

Barbecued
Charcoal barbecues provide a smoky flavour, but gas ones are easier to use. To check the heat level of your barbecue after preheating, hold your hand about 2.5 cm/1 inch above the cooking grate. The time it takes to get uncomfortably hot determines how hot the grill is:

high: about 3 seconds
medium-high: about 5 seconds
medium: about 7 seconds

Smoked
A foil pouch of wood chips creates smoke that infuses its flavour into burgers cooking in a covered barbecue (see page 94). Different kinds of wood create different flavours, so experiment. Smoking on a barbecue requires a barbecue with a lid or hood.

Grilled
Grilling is an easy, low-mess method that works especially well for fish, poultry or vegetarian burgers, which tend to stick to the grill. It is also a great alternative for any recipe that calls for grilling when the weather doesn't say 'outdoor cooking'.

HINTS AND TIPS

Choose meat with the right amount of fat. Because burgers cook over a relatively high heat, using lean meat can result in dry, tasteless burgers. The preferred fat amount for beef is 18-22 per cent, and turkey or chicken mince from leg meat is the best choice for poultry burgers when it comes to flavour and texture.

YOU CAN MINCE ALMOST ANY KIND OF FRESH MEAT YOURSELF. BEYOND THE STEAKHOUSE BURGERS (SEE PAGE 92), WHICH ARE MADE WITH BEEF, YOU CAN USE THE SAME METHOD WITH CHICKEN, LAMB, PORK OR TURKEY. JUST CUT THE MEAT INTO 2.5-CM/1-INCH CUBES AND CHILL FIRST TO AVOID ENDING UP WITH PURÉED MEAT (THIS IS PARTICULARLY IMPORTANT WITH POULTRY).

BE GENTLE WITH THE MEAT. IF YOUR BURGERS COME OUT A BIT TOUGH, IT MEANS THAT YOU PROBABLY HANDLED THE MEAT TOO MUCH WHEN FORMING THE PATTIES.

If you prefer your burgers well done, add grated cheese or finely chopped vegetables to the meat to keep it moist. Some people even add chipped ice to their mince, around 2 crushed ice cubes per 450 g/1 lb of meat (these would need to be cooked immediately, for obvious reasons).

CHOOSE YOUR BUNS WISELY. MOST BURGER AFICIONADOS PREFER SOFTER BUNS OR BREAD THAT DOESN'T FIGHT WITH THE MEAT OR VEGETABLE PATTY. IF YOU LIKE TO WARM THE BUNS, DON'T ALLOW THEM TO GET TOO DRY AND TOASTY, WITH A FEW EXCEPTIONS, SUCH AS THE PATTY MELTS (SEE PAGE 56).

Preheat. Whether using a frying pan, grill or barbecue, make sure the cooking surface or grill is very hot before you add the burgers. This will prevent sticking and result in the best browning.

Don't mess with the burgers. Some cooks like to flip their burgers several times and can't help but press down on them with a spatula. This will only toughen them up.

A FEW RECIPES CALL FOR AN ITEM ON THE BARBECUE TO BE COVERED. IN THESE INSTANCES IT IS BEST TO USE A BARBECUE THAT HAS A FITTED LID OR HOOD. ULTIMATELY, THIS FEATURE ENABLES AN INTENSE SMOKY FLAVOUR TO PENETRATE THE FOOD AND ALSO ENSURES MORE EVEN COOKING. A BARBECUE WITH A LID OR HOOD IS ESPECIALLY RECOMMENDED FOR PULLED PORK BURGERS (SEE PAGE 66) AND SMOKED BURGERS (SEE PAGE 94).

If your burger isn't binding – this can be a problem especially with poultry, fish or vegetarian burgers – try adding breadcrumbs to the mixture. Chill the formed burgers for 15 minutes to help them stay together.

CHAPTER 1
THE TIMELESS
ORIGINALS

THE CLASSIC BURGER

PREP TIME: *15 minutes, plus chilling*   **COOK TIME:** *20 minutes*

NO BARBECUE IS COMPLETE WITHOUT THE CLASSIC BEEF BURGER. THESE ARE SEASONED WITH ONION, GARLIC AND MUSTARD, BUT YOU CAN MAKE THEM IN THE PURE TRADITION OF STEAK, SALT AND PEPPER, IF YOU WISH.

MAKES 4–6

450 g/1 lb lean rump steak or topside, freshly minced

1 onion, grated

2–4 garlic cloves, crushed

2 tsp wholegrain mustard

2 tbsp sunflower oil

pepper

4–6 burger buns, split

home-made tomato ketchup (see page 170)

Chips, to serve (see page 206)

FRIED ONIONS

2 tbsp olive oil

450 g/1 lb onions, finely sliced

2 tsp light muscovado sugar

1. Preheat the barbecue. Place the minced steak, onion, garlic, mustard and pepper to taste in a large bowl and mix together thoroughly, squeezing the meat with your hand. Shape into four to six equal-sized patties, then cover and leave to chill in the refrigerator for 30 minutes.

2. Meanwhile, make the fried onions. Heat the olive oil in a heavy-based frying pan, add the onions and sauté over a low heat until soft. Add the sugar and cook for a further 8 minutes, stirring occasionally, or until the onions have caramelized. Drain well on kitchen paper and keep warm.

3. To cook the burgers on the barbecue, check they are very firm and brush generously with oil. Cook for about 5 minutes on each side or until cooked to your liking. Place the burger buns on the preheated barbecue, cut side down until lightly toasted. Place the burgers in the buns and top with the onions. Serve immediately with tomato ketchup and chips.

CLASSIC CHEESEBURGERS

PREP TIME: *10 minutes*   **COOK TIME:** *12 minutes*

MAKES 4

750 g/1 lb 10 oz fresh beef mince

1 beef stock cube

1 tbsp minced dried onion

2 tbsp water

1-2 tbsp sunflower oil

55 g/2 oz Cheddar cheese, grated

lettuce leaves

4 burger buns, split

tomato slices

chips, to serve (see page 206)

1. Place the beef in a large mixing bowl. Crumble the stock cube over the meat, add the dried onion and water and mix well. Divide the meat into four portions, shape each into a ball, then flatten slightly to make a patty of your preferred thickness.

2. Place a griddle pan over a medium-high heat. Lightly brush the burgers with oil and cook for 5-6 minutes. Turn the burgers, sprinkle the cheese over the cooked side and cook for a further 5-6 minutes, or until cooked to your liking.

3. Place the lettuce leaves on the bottom halves of the buns and top with the burgers. Place a couple of tomato slices on top and add the lids. Serve immediately with chips.

STEP 1

STEP 2

STEP 3

FOR AN EXTRA SPICY KICK TO THIS CLASSIC CHEESEBURGER, PLACE A GOOD SPOONFUL OF ENGLISH MUSTARD ON TOP OF THE COOKED BURGER BEFORE ADDING THE CHEESE.

17

TOFU BURGERS WITH CORIANDER AÏOLI

PREP TIME: *15 minutes, plus marinating*

COOK TIME: *6 minutes*

A STANDARD 280-G/10-OZ PACKET OF TOFU MAKES ENOUGH FOR ABOUT THREE BURGERS, BUT YOU CAN EASILY DOUBLE THE RECIPE.

MAKES 3

280 g/10 oz firm tofu
2 tbsp soy sauce
½ tsp Worcestershire sauce
1 garlic clove, finely chopped
¼ tsp red pepper flakes
8 small fresh coriander sprigs, roughly chopped
50 ml/2 fl oz mayonnaise
3 burger buns, split
red onion slices
lettuce leaves

1. Preheat the grill to high and place the rack about 15 cm/6 inches below the heat. Line the grill pan with foil.

2. Drain the tofu and pat dry. Slice into 1-cm/½-inch thick slabs that will roughly fit in the buns and drain on kitchen paper.

3. Combine the soy sauce, Worcestershire sauce, half the garlic and the red pepper flakes in a shallow dish wide enough to fit the tofu in a single layer. Place the tofu in the mixture, then turn to coat on both sides. Place in the refrigerator and marinate for at least 15 minutes or for up to 3 hours.

4. Put the coriander and the remaining garlic into a small food processor or blender and purée. Add the mayonnaise and mix until smooth.

5. Transfer the tofu to the prepared pan. Cook under the preheated grill for 3 minutes on each side, or until brown.

6. Spread the coriander aïoli on both halves of the buns, then add one third of the tofu to each of the bun bases. Add the onion and lettuce, finish with the top halves of the buns, slice in half and serve immediately.

19

CHEESE & BACON BURGERS

PREP TIME: 15 minutes   **COOK TIME: less than 20 minutes**

THIS AMERICAN DINER STANDBY FEATURES THE HARD-TO-BEAT COMBINATION OF BEEF, BACON AND CHEESE.

MAKES 4

6 bacon rashers
450 g/1 lb fresh beef mince
Cheddar cheese slices
4 burger buns, split
2 tbsp mayonnaise
lettuce leaves
tomato slices
salt and pepper

1. Preheat the barbecue to medium-high. Put the bacon in a frying pan over a medium heat and cook for about 8 minutes, or until crisp. Drain on kitchen paper and break the rashers in half.

2. Place the beef in a bowl and season to taste with the salt and pepper. Divide into four equal-sized portions and shape each portion into a patty.

3. Place the patties on the rack and cook, covered, for 4 minutes. Turn, top each burger with a slice of cheese, re-cover and cook for a further 4 minutes, or until the burgers are cooked to your liking and the cheese is melted.

4. Spread both halves of the buns with mayonnaise, then place each burger on a bun base. Top with the bacon pieces, lettuce and tomato slices and finish with the top halves of the buns. Serve immediately.

IF YOU LIKE YOUR BURGERS
WITH A LITTLE SPICY KICK,
WHY NOT ADD SOME
HOME-MADE CHIPOTLE KETCHUP
(SEE PAGE 180)

TURKEY BURGERS

PREP TIME: 10 minutes   COOK TIME: 5 minutes

LOW IN FAT BUT PACKED FULL OF FLAVOUR, TURKEY BURGERS MAKE A DELIGHTFUL CHANGE FROM THEIR BEEFY COUSINS AND WILL BE POPULAR WITH ALL THE FAMILY.

MAKES 4

350 g/12 oz fresh minced turkey breast

4 tbsp fresh wholemeal breadcrumbs

1 small onion, finely chopped

1 eating apple, peeled, cored and finely chopped

grated rind and juice of 1 small lemon

2 tbsp finely chopped fresh parsley

sunflower oil, for brushing

salt and pepper

4 granary rolls or focaccia, split

1. Preheat the grill to medium-high and line the grill pan with foil. Place the turkey, breadcrumbs, onion, apple, lemon rind and juice and parsley into a large bowl. Season to taste with salt and pepper and gently mix to combine. Divide into four equal-sized portions and shape each portion into a patty.

2. Brush the patties with oil and place onto the preheated grill. Cook, turning once, for 5 minutes, or until cooked through. Test to check that the juices run clear when they are pierced with the point of a knife. If there are any traces of pink, return to the grill for 1–2 minutes.

3. Place a burger on each bun base, add the bun lids and serve immediately.

STEP 2

STEP 1

THESE BURGERS ARE SLIGHTLY
MORE FRAGILE THAN BEEF
BURGERS, SO HANDLE THEM WITH
CARE WHEN PLACING ON THE
GRILL AND TURNING THEM.

THE CLASSIC CHICKEN BURGER

PREP TIME: *15–20 minutes, plus chilling* **COOK TIME:** *15–20 minutes*

MAKES 4

4 large skinless, boneless chicken breasts

1 large egg white

1 tbsp cornflour

1 tbsp plain flour

1 egg, beaten

55 g/2 oz fresh white breadcrumbs

2 tbsp sunflower oil

shredded lettuce leaves

4 burger buns, split

beef tomato slices

4 tbsp mayonnaise

chips (see page 206), to serve

1. Place the chicken breasts between two sheets of non-stick baking paper and flatten slightly using a meat mallet or a rolling pin. Beat the egg white and cornflour together, then brush over the chicken. Cover and leave to chill in the refrigerator for 30 minutes, then coat in the flour.

2. Place the egg and breadcrumbs in two separate bowls and coat the chicken first in the egg, allowing any excess to drip back into the bowl, then in the breadcrumbs.

3. Heat a heavy-based frying pan and add the oil. When hot, add the burgers and cook over a medium heat for 6–8 minutes on each side, or until thoroughly cooked. Add the tomato slices for the last 1–2 minutes of the cooking time to heat through.

4. Place some lettuce and a burger on each bun base, top with the tomatoes and a spoonful of mayonnaise. Serve immediately with chips.

HIS CLASSIC BURGER IS A FIRM
AVOURITE WITH CHICKEN AND
BURGER ENTHUSIASTS ALIKE,
AND FOR THOSE WHO LIKE TO
ATCH WHAT THEY EAT, CHICKEN
BURGERS ARE LOWER IN FAT
THAN BEEF VARIETIES.

THE CLASSIC VEGGIE BURGER

PREP TIME: 10 minutes, plus chilling   **COOK TIME: 35 minutes**

MAKES 4-6

85 g/3 oz brown rice

400 g/14 oz canned flageolet beans, drained and rinsed

115 g/4 oz unsalted cashew nuts

3 garlic cloves

1 red onion, cut into wedges

115 g/4 oz sweetcorn kernels

2 tbsp tomato purée

1 tbsp chopped fresh oregano

2 tbsp wholemeal flour

2 tbsp sunflower oil

salt and pepper

shredded lettuce leaves

4–6 wholemeal buns, split

tomato slices

halloumi cheese slices

1. Cook the rice in a saucepan of lightly salted boiling water for 20 minutes, or until tender. Drain and place in a food processor or blender.

2. Add the beans, cashew nuts, garlic, onion, sweetcorn, tomato purée, oregano and salt and pepper to taste to the rice in the food processor and, using the pulse button, blend together. Shape into four to six equal-sized patties, then coat in the flour. Cover and leave to chill in the refrigerator for 1 hour.

3. Preheat the barbecue. Brush the burgers with the oil and cook over medium-hot coals for 5–6 minutes on each side, or until cooked through.

4. Place the shredded lettuce leaves on the bottom halves of the buns and top with the burgers. Top each with one or two tomato slices and a cheese slice. Place under a hot grill for 2 minutes, until the cheese begins to melt. Add the bun lids and serve immediately.

This is a fantastic burger for vegetarians and non-vegetarians alike, full of flavour, texture and healthy ingredients. You can, if you like, substitute the flageolet beans for black-eyed or red kidney beans.

THE EVERYTHING BURGER

PREP TIME: 15 minutes   **COOK TIME:** less than 10 minutes

THIS CHEESEBURGER INCLUDES JALAPEÑO CHILLIES AND COLESLAW ALONG WITH SOME OF THE OTHER TRADITIONAL BURGER CONDIMENTS.

MAKES 4

450 g/1 lb fresh beef mince
1 tsp salt
½ tsp pepper
vegetable oil, for frying
Cheddar cheese slices
4 soft burger buns, split
mustard, for spreading
Pickled Jalapeños
(see page 198)
Coleslaw (see page 176)
tomato slices

1. Place the mince into a medium-sized bowl with the salt and pepper and gently mix to combine, then divide into four equal-sized portions and shape each portion into a patty.

2. Place a large frying pan or ridged griddle pan over a medium–high heat and add enough oil to coat the base of the pan. Add the patties, partially cover and cook for about 4 minutes, without moving, until the burgers are brown and release easily from the pan. Turn, place a slice of cheese on top of each burger, partially cover again and cook for a further 3 minutes, or until cooked to your liking.

3. Spread the mustard on both halves of the buns and place a few slices of pickled jalapeños on each bun base. Set a burger on top of each base, add some coleslaw and a tomato slice, and serve immediately.

You can add as little or as much as you like to this all-American burger. For something a bit different, why not try home-made chipotle mustard (see page 180)

29

DOUBLE-DECKER BURGERS

PREP TIME: *20 minutes*   **COOK TIME:** *less than 10 minutes*

ALSO CALLED A 'DOUBLE' AT FAST-FOOD RESTAURANTS,
A DOUBLE-DECKER STACKS TWO BEEF PATTIES FOR
A HUGE MOUTHFUL OF A BURGER.

MAKES 4

900 g/2 lb fresh beef mince
2 tsp salt
½ tsp pepper
vegetable oil, for frying
Cheddar cheese slices
4 soft burger buns
lettuce leaves
tomato slices
red onion slices
gherkins, halved lengthways

1. Place the beef in a medium-sized bowl with the salt and pepper and mix gently to combine. Divide into eight equal-sized portions and shape each portion into a patty no thicker than 1 cm/½ inch – the thinner the better for these burgers.

2. Place a large griddle pan over a medium-high heat. Add enough oil to coat the base of the pan. Add the patties and cook for about 4 minutes, without moving, until the burgers are brown and release easily from the pan. Turn and cook on the other side for 2 minutes, then put a slice of cheese on top of each burger and cook for a further 2 minutes, or until cooked to your liking.

3. Place a burger on each bun base, then place a second burger on top. Add the lettuce leaves, tomato slices, onion slices and gherkins and serve immediately.

STEP 2

STEP 1

TO MAKE THIS BURGER MORE MANAGEABLE, MAKE SURE THAT THE PATTIES ARE NOT TOO BIG OR TOO THICK.

BLUE CHEESE & ONION BURGERS

PREP TIME: *15 minutes*   **COOK TIME:** *less than 10 minutes*

A CROWN OF MELTING BLUE CHEESE AND RED ONION RINGS MAKE THIS BURGER DISTINCTIVE.

MAKES 4

450 g/1 lb fresh beef mince
1 tsp salt
½ tsp pepper
vegetable oil, for brushing
4 burger buns, split
55 g/2 oz blue cheese, crumbled
lettuce leaves
red onion slices

1. Preheat the grill to high. Place the grill rack 5–8 cm/2–3¼ inches below the heat.

2. Place the mince into a medium-sized bowl with the salt and pepper and mix gently to combine, then divide into four equal-sized portions and shape each portion into a patty.

3. Brush the patties with oil, place on the rack and cook for about 4 minutes on each side, or until cooked to your liking.

4. Place the burgers in the buns. Put some cheese on top of each burger, pressing it down slightly to hold its shape. Top with the lettuce and onions and serve immediately.

STEP 2

STEP 3

STEP 4

BLUE CHEESE HAS A DISTINCTIVE LOOK AND SMELL AND CAN ALSO VARY CONSIDERABLY IN STRENGTH.

MUSHROOM-SWISS BURGERS

PREP TIME: *30 minutes*   **COOK TIME:** *15 minutes*

IT'S HARD TO BEAT THE CLASSIC COMBINATION OF SAUTÉED MUSHROOMS AND GRUYÈRE CHEESE ON TOP OF A GRIDDLED BURGER.

MAKES 4

2 tsp vegetable oil, plus extra for brushing

½ yellow onion, thinly sliced

115 g/4 oz mushrooms, sliced

450 g/1 lb fresh beef mince

1 tsp salt

½ tsp pepper

Gruyère cheese slices

4 poppy seed buns, split

lettuce leaves

tomato slices

salt and pepper

1. Heat the oil in a medium-sized frying pan over a medium–high heat. Add the onion and cook for 3 minutes, stirring, until soft. Add the mushrooms and season to taste with salt and pepper. Cook for 1–2 minutes, then stir. Continue to cook until the mushrooms are cooked through.

2. Place the beef in a bowl, add 1 teaspoon salt and ½ teaspoon pepper and gently mix to combine. Divide into four equal-sized portions and shape each portion into a patty.

3. Heat a griddle pan over a medium–high heat, then brush with oil. Add the patties and cover the pan. Cook for about 4 minutes until brown, then turn and cook on the other side for 2 minutes. Add the cheese and cook for a further 2 minutes, or until cooked to your liking.

4. Place the lettuce and tomato slices on each bun base then top with the burgers. Add the mushroom mixture and top halves of the buns and serve immediately.

35

CHILLI BURGERS

PREP TIME: 15 minutes   **COOK TIME:** less than 10 minutes

THIS BEEF EXTRAVAGANZA OF A BURGER SMOTHERED IN BEEF CHILLI STEW AND CHEESE ORIGINALLY CAME FROM A DINER IN LOS ANGELES.

MAKES 4

450 g/1 lb fresh beef mince
1 tsp salt
½ tsp pepper
1 tbsp butter
4 soft burger buns, split
½ quantity Beef Chilli (see page 194), warmed
red onion slices
30–55 g/1–2 oz Cheddar cheese, grated

1. Place the mince into a medium-sized bowl, add the salt and pepper and mix gently to combine. Divide into four equal-sized portions and shape each portion into a patty.

2. Heat a large frying pan over a medium–high heat. Melt the butter in the pan and heat until it has stopped foaming. Add the patties and cook for about 4 minutes, without moving, until they are brown and release easily from the pan. Turn and cook on the other side for a further 4 minutes, or until cooked to your liking.

3. Place the open buns on plates. Set each burger on a bun and ladle just enough beef chilli on top to cover, then sprinkle with the onion and cheese. Serve immediately.

KA-POW!

THIS IS ONE BURGER YOU MAY NEED TO EAT WITH A FORK!

CARAMELIZED ONION BURGERS

PREP TIME: 15 minutes   COOK TIME: less than 10 minutes

ROSEMARY-SCENTED BURGERS GET DRESSED UP WITH SILKY CARAMELIZED ONIONS, FOCACCIA AND MATURE MANCHEGO CHEESE.

MAKES 4

450 g/1 lb fresh beef mince

1 tsp salt

½ tsp pepper

½ tsp finely chopped fresh rosemary

vegetable oil, for frying

55-85 g/2-3 oz Manchego cheese, grated or thinly sliced

125 ml/4 fl oz mayonnaise

4 x 15-cm/6-inch square pieces focaccia, split

Caramelized Onions (see page 202)

cos lettuce leaves

tomato slices

1. Place the beef in a medium-sized bowl with the salt, pepper and rosemary and gently mix to combine, then divide into four equal-sized portions and shape each portion into a patty.

2. Place a large frying pan or ridged griddle pan over a medium-high heat. Add enough oil to coat the base of the pan. Add the patties and cook for about 4 minutes, without moving, until the burgers are brown and release easily from the pan. Turn and cook for 2 minutes, then place some cheese on top of each burger and cook for a further 2 minutes, or until cooked to your liking.

3. Spread the mayonnaise on the focaccia. Place the burgers on the bottom pieces of the foccacia, top with the caramelized onions, lettuce leaves and tomato slices, add the lids and serve immediately.

STEP 2

STEP 2

STEP 3

FOCACCIA; A FLAT OVEN-BAKED ITALIAN BREAD, MAKES A DELICIOUS ALTERNATIVE TO THE CLASSIC BURGER BUN.

SLOPPY JOES

PREP TIME: 10 minutes   COOK TIME: 1 hour

THE SECRET TO A GREAT SLOPPY JOE IS SLOWLY
SIMMERING THE BEEF MIXTURE UNTIL IT'S RICH AND TENDER.
BY THE WAY, YOU SHOULD ALWAYS SERVE SLOPPY JOES
WITH A FORK, BUT YOU SHOULD NEVER NEED TO USE IT!

MAKES 4-6

675 g/1 lb 8 oz lean beef mince

½ onion, diced

2 garlic cloves, finely chopped

1 green pepper, diced

450 ml/16 fl oz water

175 ml/6 fl oz tomato ketchup

1½ tbsp soft light brown sugar

1 tsp Dijon mustard

dash of Worcestershire sauce

1½ tsp salt

½ tsp black pepper

cayenne pepper, to taste

4-6 burger buns, split

crisps, to serve (optional)

1. Put the beef and onions into a large cold frying pan and place over a medium heat. Cook, stirring, breaking up the meat into very small pieces with a wooden spoon, until it begins to brown.

2. Add the garlic and green pepper and cook, stirring, for 2 minutes. Add half the water. Cook until simmering, scraping up any sediment from the base of the pan.

3. Stir in the tomato ketchup, sugar, mustard, Worcestershire sauce, salt, black pepper, cayenne pepper and the remaining water. Bring to simmering point, reduce the heat to low, and simmer for 30-45 minutes, or until most of the liquid has evaporated and the meat mixture is thick, rich and tender. Spoon the beef mixture onto each bun base. Add the bun lids and serve immediately with crisps, if desired.

THESE BURGERS ARE ALWAYS SERVED HOT, BUT THE SLOPPY JOE MIXTURE CAN BE MADE IN ADVANCE AND REHEATED. MAKE DOUBLE THE QUANTITY, IT CAN BE FROZEN FOR UP TO THREE MONTHS.

BEAN BURGERS

PREP TIME: *15 minutes*   COOK TIME: *10–12 minutes*

MAKES 4

425 g/15 oz canned red kidney beans, drained and rinsed

410 g/14½ oz canned cooked chickpeas, drained and rinsed

1 egg yolk

¼ tsp smoked paprika

50 g/1¾ oz fresh breadcrumbs

3 spring onions, finely chopped

oil for brushing

salt and pepper

4 crusty bread rolls, split

4 tbsp soured cream

lettuce leaves

tomato slices

1. Preheat the barbecue to high.

2. Place the beans, chickpeas, egg yolk, paprika, breadcrumbs and spring onions in a large bowl and gently mix to combine. Season to taste with salt and pepper. Divide the mixture into four equal-sized portions and shape each portion into a patty. Season the outside of the patties with salt and pepper and lightly brush with oil.

3. Oil the barbecue rack. Cook the burgers for 5 minutes on each side, or until cooked through. Brush the inside of the buns with oil and toast over the barbecue, cut-side down, for 1–2 minutes. Place the lettuce and tomato on each bun base, then top with the burgers and soured cream. Add the bun lids and serve immediately.

IF THE BURGERS DO NOT HOLD TOGETHER WHEN YOU TRY TO SHAPE THEM, ADD JUST A LITTLE MORE OIL TO THE MIXTURE TO MAKE THEM EASIER TO HANDLE.

BARBECUE BURGERS

PREP TIME: 15 minutes   COOK TIME: less than 10 minutes

THIS SIMPLE BURGER FEATURES BARBECUE SAUCE; FOR EVEN MORE AUTHENTIC FLAVOUR, TRY SMOKING YOUR BURGERS (SEE PAGE 94).

MAKES 4

450 g/1 lb fresh beef mince
1 tsp salt
½ tsp pepper
30 g/1 oz finely chopped onion
1 garlic clove, finely chopped
175 ml/6 fl oz Barbecue Sauce (see page 172)
4 soft burger buns, split
lettuce leaves
tomato slices

1. Preheat the barbecue to medium-high. Place the mince into a medium-sized bowl with the salt, pepper, onion and garlic and mix gently to combine. Divide into four equal portions and shape each portion into a patty.

2. Place 125 ml/4 fl oz of the barbecue sauce in a bowl.

3. Put the patties on the rack and cook for 4 minutes until brown on one side. Turn, baste with the barbecue sauce and cook for a further 4 minutes, or until cooked to your liking.

4. Spread some of the remaining barbecue sauce on the buns, then place the burgers in the buns. Top with the lettuce leaves and tomato slices and serve immediately.

STEP 1

STEP 3

STEP 3

IF YOU DON'T HAVE THE TIME TO MAKE YOUR OWN BARBECUE SAUCE, THERE ARE MANY EXCELLENT SHOP-BOUGHT VERSIONS YOU CAN TRY.

45

TURKEY CLUB BURGERS

PREP TIME: 20 minutes   COOK TIME: 20 minutes

TAKING A CUE FROM CLUB SANDWICHES, WHICH STACK
SLICED TURKEY WITH BACON, LETTUCE AND TOMATO
BETWEEN TOASTED BREAD, THESE BURGERS ARE
LAYERED WITH FLAVOUR.

MAKES 4

450 g/1 lb fresh turkey mince

1 garlic clove, finely chopped

1½ tsp finely chopped fresh rosemary

1 tsp salt

½ tsp pepper

6 bacon rashers

8 slices white farmhouse bread, toasted

2-3 tbsp ranch-style dressing

lettuce leaves

tomato slices

1. Preheat the barbecue to medium-high. Combine the turkey mince with the garlic, rosemary, salt and pepper in a bowl. Divide the mixture into four equal-sized portions and shape each portion into a thick patty.

2. Cook the bacon in a frying pan over a medium heat for about 8 minutes, or until crisp. Drain on kitchen paper and break the pieces in half.

3. Spread each slice of bread with about ½ a teaspoon of the ranch-style dressing.

4. Put the burgers on the rack and cook over a medium heat, covered, for 4-5 minutes on each side, or until cooked through.

5. Place each burger on a slice of the toasted bread, add the bacon, lettuce leaves and tomato slices, drizzle with a little more dressing and top with the remaining toasted bread. Serve immediately.

47

BUTTERLICIOUS BURGERS

PREP TIME: *30 minutes, plus chilling*   **COOK TIME:** *10 minutes*

THESE BURGERS CAN BE MADE WITH PLAIN BUTTER, BUT ARE BROUGHT TO A WHOLE NEW LEVEL WITH A BIT OF GARLIC AND PLENTY OF HERBS.

MAKES 4

75 g/2¾ oz butter

½ tsp finely chopped garlic

1 tbsp finely chopped fresh parsley

1 tsp each finely chopped fresh thyme, rosemary and/or sage

1½ tsp salt

450 g/1 lb fresh beef mince

4 soft burger buns, split

1. Put 4 tablespoons of the butter into a small bowl with the garlic, herbs and ½ teaspoon of the salt and gently mix to combine. Transfer the butter mixture to a piece of clingfilm and roll into a 2.5-cm/1-inch thick log. Chill in the refrigerator for at least 1 hour and up to 2 days.

2. When ready to make the burgers, remove the butter log from the refrigerator, cut into four equal-sized slices and set aside to return to room temperature.

3. Combine the mince and the remaining salt in a large bowl. Divide into four equal-sized portions and shape each portion into a patty.

4. Heat a large frying pan over a medium-high heat. Add the remaining butter and heat until foaming. When it has stopped foaming add the burgers and cook for about 4 minutes, without moving, until the burgers are brown and come away easily from the pan. Turn and cook for a further 4 minutes on the other side, until cooked to your liking.

5. Place a burger on each bun base. Top with the seasoned butter, add the bun lids and serve immediately.

YOU CAN VARY THE HERBS USED IN YOUR BUTTER MIXTURE TO YOUR LIKING. PARSLEY, OREGANO, CHIVES, BASIL AND TARRAGON ALL WORK WELL, OR ADD A LITTLE FRESH RED CHILLI FOR A SPICIER VERSION.

49

LAMB & MINT BURGERS

PREP TIME: 10 minutes, plus chilling **COOK TIME:** 20-25 minutes

MAKES 4-6

2 tbsp olive oil

1 red pepper, deseeded and cut into quarters

1 yellow pepper, deseeded and cut into quarters

1 red onion, cut into thick wedges

1 baby aubergine (115 g/4 oz), cut into wedges

450 g/1 lb fresh lamb mince

2 tbsp freshly grated Parmesan cheese

1 tbsp chopped fresh mint

salt and pepper

4-6 burger buns, split

shredded lettuce leaves

grilled vegetables, such as peppers and cherry tomatoes, to serve

MINTY MUSTARD MAYONNAISE

4 tbsp mayonnaise

1 tsp Dijon mustard

1 tbsp chopped fresh mint

1. Preheat the barbecue to medium-hot. Oil the barbecue rack.

2. Place the peppers, onions and aubergine on the rack and cook over hot coals for 10-12 minutes, or until charred. Remove, leave to cool, then peel the peppers.

3. Place all the barbecued vegetables in a food processor or blender and, using the pulse button, chop. Add the lamb mince, Parmesan cheese, chopped mint and salt and pepper to taste to the food processor and blend until combined. Divide the mixture into 4-6 balls and flatten into patties about 2.5 cm/1 inch thick. Season the outside with salt and pepper, and lightly brush with oil.

4. Next make the minty mustard mayonnaise. Blend the mayonnaise with the mustard and chopped fresh mint. Cover and chill in the refrigerator until required.

5. Place the burgers over hot coals and cook for 5 minutes on each side, or until cooked through. Brush the inside of the buns with oil and toast over the barbecue, cut-side down, for 1-2 minutes. Place the burgers in the buns with the shredded lettuce, prepared mayonnaise and barbecued vegetables. Serve immediately.

LAMB AND FRESH MINT ARE A
CLASSIC PARTNERSHIP, WHICH IS
GREATLY ENHANCED HERE BY THE
INTRODUCTION OF SWEET
PEPPERS, RICH AUBERGINE
AND A LITTLE PUNGENT
PARMESAN CHEESE.

BACON-WRAPPED CHICKEN BURGERS

PREP TIME: 10 minutes, plus chilling

COOK TIME: 10–15 minutes

MAKES 4

450 g/1 lb fresh chicken mince
1 onion, grated
2 garlic cloves, crushed
55 g/2 oz pine nuts, toasted
55 g/2 oz Gruyère cheese, grated
2 tbsp fresh snipped chives
2 tbsp wholemeal flour
8 slices lean back bacon
1–2 tbsp sunflower oil
salt and pepper
4 crusty rolls, split
red onion slices
lettuce leaves
4 tbsp mayonnaise
spring onions, chopped

1. Place the chicken mince, onion, garlic, pine nuts, Gruyère cheese, chives and salt and pepper in a food processor or blender. Using the pulse button, blend the mixture together using short sharp bursts. Scrape out onto a board and shape into four even-sized burgers. Coat in the flour, then cover and chill in the refrigerator for 1 hour.

2. Wrap each burger with two bacon slices, securing in place with a wooden cocktail stick.

3. Heat a heavy-based frying pan over a medium heat and add the oil. When hot, add the burgers and cook over a medium heat for 5–6 minutes on each side, or until cooked through.

4. Serve the burgers in the crusty rolls with the red onion, lettuce, a spoonful of mayonnaise and spring onions. Serve immediately.

You can alter the flavour and texture of these luscious burgers by replacing the pine nuts with flaked almonds or unsalted cashews. If using whole nuts, chop them first and, if liked, toast lightly.

GREEN CHILLI BURGERS

PREP TIME: *20 minutes, plus chilling*   **COOK TIME:** *45 minutes*

GREEN CHILLI BURGERS ARE COMMON IN THE PUEBLO AND COLORADO SPRINGS AREA OF COLORADO. EVEN THOUGH THEY'RE SERVED ON A BUN, THEY DEFINITELY REQUIRE A KNIFE AND FORK!

MAKES 4

8 poblano chillies
2 onions
3 garlic cloves
1 tbsp vegetable oil
1½ tsp salt
900 g/2 lb fresh beef mince
4 burger buns, split
Cheddar cheese slices

1. Preheat the barbecue to high. Place the chillies on the rack and cook, turning occasionally, until the skin is blackened. Set aside for about 15 minutes, or until cool enough to handle.

2. Meanwhile, finely chop the onions and garlic. Peel and chop the chillies.

3. Put the oil, three quarters of the chopped onion and ½ teaspoon of the salt into a medium-sized saucepan over a high heat and cook, stirring frequently, for about 3 minutes, or until soft. Add the garlic and chillies, cover, reduce the heat to low and cook for about 30 minutes, or until the flavours have blended and the vegetables are all soft. Set aside.

4. Place the beef and the remaining salt in a large bowl and gently mix to combine. Divide into four equal-sized portions and shape each portion into a patty. Cover and chill in the refrigerator.

5. Place the buns cut side down on the rack and toast for 1–2 minutes. Transfer the buns to plates.

6. Place the patties on the rack and cook for about 4 minutes until brown, then flip and cook on the other side. After 2 minutes, put a slice of cheese on top of each burger, cover and cook for about 3 minutes, or until the burgers are cooked to your liking and the cheese is melted.

7. Place a burger on each bun base. Top with the green chilli sauce and the remaining chopped onion, add the bun lids and serve immediately.

STEP 6

STEP 1

POBLANO CHILLIES CAN BE FOUND IN SPECIALTY STORES, HOWEVER, YOU CAN ALSO USE ANY CHILLI OF YOUR CHOICE – JUST REMEMBER THAT CHILLIES CAN VARY HUGELY IN BOTH SIZE AND HEAT!

PATTY MELTS

PREP TIME: 20 minutes   **COOK TIME:** 12 minutes

A PATTY MELT TAKES TWO CLASSIC SANDWICHES – BURGER AND TOASTED CHEESE – AND PUTS THEM TOGETHER WITH RYE BREAD AND CARAMELIZED ONIONS.

MAKES 4

2 tbsp softened butter, plus extra for greasing

8 slices light rye bread

8 thin slices Cheddar cheese

600 g/1 lb 5 oz fresh beef mince

1 tsp salt

½ tsp pepper

1 quantity Caramelized Onions (see page 202)

1. Spread the butter on the bread. Place four slices buttered side down on a clean work surface. Top each slice with one slice of cheese.

2. Place the beef into a bowl, add the salt and pepper and combine. Divide into four equal-sized portions and shape each portion into a rectangular patty.

3. Grease a griddle pan with butter and heat over a medium heat. Add the patties to the pan and cook for about 4 minutes on each side, or until cooked to your liking. Wipe the pan clean.

4. Place the burgers on top of the cheese-topped bread slices, then add the caramelized onions and the remaining cheese slices. Top with the remaining bread slices, buttered side up.

5. Place the sandwiches in the wiped pan and cook over a medium heat for 2 minutes on each side, or until golden brown. Serve immediately.

CHEESE AND ONION IS A WELL-KNOWN AND DELICIOUS COMBINATION OF INGREDIENTS. YOU CAN BUY CARAMELIZED ONIONS FROM MOST GOOD SUPERMARKETS AND ALSO VARY THE CHEESE USED TO SUIT YOUR TASTES.

THE ORIGINAL FISH BURGER

PREP TIME: 10 minutes   **COOK TIME:** 10 minutes

THIS FISH BURGER IS A CLASSIC ON HAWAIIAN MENUS, WHERE IT IS OFTEN MADE WITH MAHI MAHI. OTHER WHITE FISH, SUCH AS POLLACK OR TILAPIA WORK PERFECTLY WHEN MAHI MAHI ISN'T AVAILABLE.

MAKES 4

4 x 115–175-g/4–6-oz mahi mahi or other white fish fillets

2 tsp vegetable or rapeseed oil

$\frac{1}{2}$ tsp sea salt

$\frac{1}{4}$ tsp pepper

4 soft burger buns, split

4 tbsp Tartare Sauce (see page 182)

onion slices

lettuce leaves

tomato slices

1. Rinse the fish and pat dry. Rub the fillets on both sides with the oil and sprinkle with the salt and pepper. Place on a large baking sheet.

2. Preheat the grill to high and place the rack about 8 cm/3$\frac{1}{4}$ inches below the heat.

3. Place the fish on the rack and cook under the preheated grill for 4 minutes, then turn and cook for a further 3 minutes, or until the edges start to brown and the fish is just cooked through (the centre of the fish should flake easily when cut into).

4. Spread both halves of each bun with the tartare sauce. Place a fish fillet on each bun base and top with the onion slices, lettuce leaves and tomato slices. Add the bun lids and serve immediately.

FOR A TRULY HAWAIIAN FEEL, TOP THESE BURGERS WITH SOME JUICY PINEAPPLE RINGS.

CHEESE-STUFFED BURGERS

PREP TIME: *20 minutes*   COOK TIME: *15–25 minutes*

A CULT HIT IN MINNESOTA, THESE CHEESE-STUFFED
BURGERS ARE BIG ENOUGH TO ACCOMMODATE THE FILLING.
BE CAREFUL BECAUSE THE MOLTEN FILLING WILL BE VERY
HOT WHEN THE BURGERS COME OFF THE BARBECUE.

MAKES 2

325 g/11½ oz fresh beef mince
1 tsp salt
½ tsp pepper
2 slices Cheddar cheese, quartered
vegetable oil, for frying
½ red onion, sliced
2 soft burger buns, split
lettuce leaves
tomato slices

1. Preheat the barbecue to medium-high. Place the mince in a small bowl with the salt and pepper and combine. Divide into four equal-sized portions and roll each portion into a ball. Place the balls on a clean work surface and flatten until slightly larger than the buns and about 1 cm/½ inch thick. Arrange the cheese in a circle on top of two of the patties, leaving a 1-cm/½-inch border. Add the remaining two patties and firmly press the sides to seal (otherwise the cheese will come out during cooking).

2. Heat the oil in a frying pan over a medium heat. Add the onion slices and fry for about 8 minutes, stirring frequently, until soft and brown. Alternatively, you could barbecue the onion slices for about 2 minutes on each side while you cook the burgers.

3. Place the patties on the rack, rounded side up. Cook for 8 minutes, then carefully turn over and cook on the other side for 5–7 minutes.

4. Place each burger on a bun base, top with the onions, lettuce, tomatoes and the top half of the bun and serve immediately.

THE LOW-CARB BURGER

PREP TIME: 15 minutes   COOK TIME: less than 10 minutes

THESE FRESH BURGERS HAVE NO BUNS OR CHEESE TO GET IN THE WAY OF THE MEAT. THE CRISP, JUICY VEGETABLES OFFSET THE BEEF'S RICH FLAVOUR AS IT COMES OFF THE GRILL.

MAKES 4

450 g/1 lb fresh beef mince

¼ tsp dried thyme or ½ tsp chopped fresh thyme

courgette slices

vegetable oil, for brushing

lettuce leaves

tomato slices

onion slices

salt and pepper

1. Preheat the barbecue to medium-high. Place the beef into a medium-sized bowl with ½ teaspoon of salt, ¼ teaspoon of pepper and the thyme. Gently mix to combine, then divide into four equal-sized portions and shape each portion into a patty.

2. Lightly brush the courgette slices with oil and sprinkle with salt and pepper.

3. Place the patties and courgette slices on the rack. Cook the courgette slices for about 3 minutes on each side until soft and marked. Cook the burgers for 4 minutes on each side, or until cooked to your liking.

4. Place a burger on a few lettuce leaves. Top with the courgette, tomato and onion slices, then wrap the lettuce over to encase the burger. Serve immediately.

THIS BURGER IS PERFECT IF YOU ARE TRYING TO CUT DOWN ON CARBOHYDRATES IN YOUR DIET AS IT'S COMPLETELY BREAD-FREE!

CHAPTER 2
THE GOURMET
SHOW-STOPPERS

PULLED PORK BURGERS

PREP TIME: *20 minutes, plus standing*   **COOK TIME:** *6 hours*

SLOW-COOKED PORK 'PULLED' INTO SHREDS AND TOPPED WITH SWEET-YET-VINEGARY SAUCE MAKES IRRESISTIBLE BURGER-LIKE SANDWICHES.

SERVES 12

1 pork shoulder, about 2.25 kg/5 lb

30 g/1 oz paprika

50 g/1¾ oz soft dark brown sugar

2 tbsp salt

2 tbsp pepper

2 tbsp ground cumin

2 tbsp mustard powder

1 tbsp cayenne pepper

12 soft sandwich rolls, split

Home-made Pickle Relish (see page 178) and Barbecue Sauce (see page 172)

1. Prepare a barbecue for a low-medium heat by building the fire on one side only (heat only one element on a gas barbecue), then place a saucepan half-filled with water on the unlit side and set the rack over it.

2. Rinse the pork and pat dry. In a small bowl, mix the paprika, sugar, salt, pepper, cumin, mustard and cayenne pepper. Rub this spice mixture all over the pork. Use all of the mixture, making a bit of a crust on the meat.

3. Place the pork on the rack over the pan of water, cover the barbecue with a lid and cook for about 6 hours until the meat is extremely tender. Check about every 30 minutes to make sure the fire is still going, adding more fuel and water as needed.

4. Remove the meat from the barbecue and leave to stand for 10-20 minutes. Use forks or tongs to pull the pork into shreds.

5. Serve the pulled pork on a platter with the buns, pickle relish and barbecue sauce, letting everyone make their own burger.

STEP 2

STEP 3

PULLED PORK CAN BE FOUND IN MANY DIFFERENT GUISES AROUND THE WORLD YET IT IS MOST COMMONLY ASSOCIATED WITH THE US.

BLACK & BLUE BURGERS

PREP TIME: *30 minutes*   **COOK TIME:** *10 minutes*

THESE BURGERS GET THEIR NAME FROM A BLACK PEPPER
SPICE RUB AND A BLUE CHEESE DRESSING.

MAKES 4

115 g/4 oz blue cheese
50 ml/2 fl oz mayonnaise
50 ml/2 fl oz soured cream
1 shallot, finely chopped
1 tsp pepper
1 tsp paprika
1 tsp dried thyme
1 tsp salt
½ tsp cayenne pepper
450 g/1 lb fresh beef mince
4 sesame seed burger buns, split
lettuce leaves
tomato slices

1. Put the cheese, mayonnaise and soured cream into a bowl and mash together until the mixture is as smooth as possible. Add the shallot and stir it into the dressing. Set aside.

2. Mix the pepper, paprika, thyme, salt and cayenne pepper together in a small bowl.

3. Divide the meat into four equal-sized portions and shape each portion into a patty. Sprinkle evenly on both sides with the spice mixture.

4. Heat a large, non-stick frying pan over a high heat. Add the patties and cook for about 4 minutes until the spice mixture forms a light crust and the edges are brown. Turn and cook on the other side for a further 4 minutes until brown and cooked to your liking.

5. Transfer the burgers to the buns, top with the blue cheese dressing, lettuce leaves and tomato slices and serve immediately.

STEP 1

STEP 2

STEP 4

You can vary the spices used in this recipe to suit your own personal tastes. Use garlic powder, onion powder or even chilli powder to give the spice rub a whole new dimension.

69

BEETROOT BURGERS

PREP TIME: 30 minutes, plus standing and chilling

COOK TIME: 35-40 minutes

THESE WHOLESOME, CRISP BEETROOT-AND-MILLET BURGERS HAIL FROM AUSTRALIA. THE TANGY YOGURT SAUCE CONTRASTS WITH THE SWEET, EARTHY VEGETABLES.

MAKES 5

100 g/3½ oz millet
175 ml/6 fl oz lightly salted water
150 g/5½ oz raw beetroot, grated
30 g/1 oz carrots, grated
175 g/6 oz courgettes, grated
60 g/2¼ oz walnuts, finely chopped
2 tbsp cider vinegar
2 tbsp extra virgin olive oil, plus extra for frying
1 egg
2 tbsp cornflour
225 ml/8 fl oz natural yogurt
2 tsp finely chopped garlic
5 multi-grain buns, split
lettuce leaves
salt and pepper

1. Rinse and drain the millet and place in a small saucepan with the salted water. Place over a medium heat, bring to a simmer, cover and cook over a very low heat for 20-25 minutes until tender. Remove from the heat and leave to stand for 5 minutes, covered.

2. Put the beetroot, carrots, courgettes and walnuts into a large bowl. Add the millet, vinegar, oil, ½ teaspoon of salt and ¼ teaspoon of pepper and mix well. Add the egg and cornflour, mix again, then chill in the refrigerator for 2 hours.

3. Put the yogurt in a fine strainer over a bowl and drain for at least 30 minutes. Stir in the garlic and season to taste with salt and pepper.

4. Pack the beetroot mixture into a 125 ml/4 fl oz cup, then shape into a patty. Repeat to make a total of five burgers. Place a ridged griddle pan or large frying pan over a medium heat and coat with oil. Add the patties and cook for about 5 minutes on each side, turning carefully, until brown.

5. Spread the buns with the yogurt sauce and place the burgers in the buns, topped with the lettuce. Serve immediately.

USE SMALLER BEETROOTS WITH A DEEP-MAROON COLOURING, AS THEY HAVE A SWEETER TASTE AND ARE MUCH MORE TENDER. LARGER BEETROOT CAN OFTEN BE WOODY WITH A TOUGH CENTRE.

PORK BURGERS WITH ORANGE MARINADE

PREP TIME: *25 minutes, plus chilling*   **COOK TIME:** *45 minutes*

MAKES 4—6

450 g/1 lb pork fillet, cut into small pieces

3 tbsp Seville orange marmalade

2 tbsp orange juice

1 tbsp balsamic vinegar

225 g/8 oz parsnips, cut into chunks

1 tbsp finely grated orange rind

2 garlic cloves, crushed

6 spring onions, finely chopped

1 courgette, grated

1 tbsp sunflower oil

salt and pepper

lettuce leaves

4-6 burger buns, split

1. Place the pork in a shallow dish. Place the marmalade, orange juice and vinegar in a small saucepan and heat, stirring, until the marmalade is runny. Pour the marinade over the pork. Cover and leave for at least 30 minutes. Remove the pork, reserving the marinade. Mince the pork into a large bowl.

2. Meanwhile, cook the parsnips in a saucepan of boiling water for 15-20 minutes, or until tender. Drain, then mash and add to the pork. Stir in the orange rind, garlic, spring onions, courgette and salt and pepper to taste. Mix together, then shape into four to six equal-sized burgers. Cover and leave to chill in the refrigerator for at least 30 minutes.

3. Preheat the barbecue. Lightly brush each burger with the oil and then add them to the barbecue grill, cooking over medium-hot coals for 4-6 minutes on each side, or until cooked through. Boil the reserved marinade for at least 5 minutes, then pour into a small jug or bowl.

4. Place the lettuce leaves on the bottom halves of the burger buns and top with the burgers. Spoon over a little of the hot marinade, then top with the lids and serve immediately.

KA-POW!

THE PIQUANT FLAVOUR OF ORANGE JUICE AND RIND IS THE MAKING OF THIS BURGER. EVEN THE LARGE PIECES OF ORANGE PEEL IN THE MARMALADE PLAY THEIR PART BY ADDING EXTRA TEXTURE.

TUNA BURGERS WITH MANGO SALSA

PREP TIME: *15 minutes, plus chilling*   **COOK TIME:** *25-35 minutes*

FRESH TUNA, CHILLI AND MANGO ARE UNITED IN A TOTALLY MODERN BURGER. TUNA IS BEST EATEN SLIGHTLY PINK AS IT CAN BE RATHER DRY IF OVERCOOKED. IT IS ALSO IMPORTANT THAT THE BURGERS ARE PIPING HOT BEFORE SERVING.

MAKES 4-6

225 g/8 oz sweet potatoes, chopped

450 g/1 lb tuna steaks

6 spring onions, finely chopped

175 g/6 oz courgettes, grated

1 fresh red jalapeño chilli, deseeded and finely chopped

2 tbsp mango chutney

1 tbsp sunflower oil

salt

lettuce leaves

MANGO SALSA

1 large ripe mango, peeled and stoned

2 ripe tomatoes, finely chopped

1 fresh red jalapeño chilli, deseeded and finely chopped

4-cm/1½-inch piece cucumber, finely diced

1 tbsp chopped fresh coriander

1-2 tsp clear honey

1. Cook the sweet potatoes in a saucepan of lightly salted boiling water for 15-20 minutes, or until tender. Drain well, then mash and place in a food processor or blender. Cut the tuna into chunks and add to the potatoes.

2. Add the spring onions, courgette, chilli, and mango chutney to the food processor and, using the pulse button, blend together. Shape into four to six equal-sized patties, then cover and chill in the refrigerator for 1 hour.

3. Meanwhile make the salsa. Slice the mango, reserving 8-12 slices for serving. Finely chop the remainder, then mix with the tomatoes, chilli, cucumber, coriander and honey. Mix well, then spoon into a small bowl. Cover and leave for 30 minutes to allow the flavours to develop.

4. Preheat the barbecue. Brush the burgers lightly with the oil and cook over hot coals for 4-6 minutes on each side, or until piping hot. Serve immediately with the mango salsa, garnished with lettuce leaves and the reserved mango slices.

STEP 1

STEP 3

THERE ARE MANY VARIATIONS OF SALSAS AND RELISHES THAT WORK PERFECTLY WITH THIS BURGER. WHY NOT TRY THE TOMATO & RED ONION RELISH (PAGE 184) OR THE SWEETCORN RELISH (PAGE 190).

BLUE CHEESE & APPLE BURGERS

PREP TIME: 12 minutes, plus chilling   **COOK TIME: 25-35 minutes**

MAKES 4-6

175 g/6 oz new potatoes

225 g/8 oz mixed nuts, such as pecans, almonds and hazelnuts

1 onion, roughly chopped

2 small eating apples, peeled, cored and grated

175 g/6 oz blue cheese, such as Stilton, crumbled

55 g/2 oz fresh wholemeal breadcrumbs

2 tbsp wholemeal flour

1-2 tbsp sunflower oil

salt and pepper

lettuce leaves

4-6 cheese-topped burger buns, split

red onion slices

1. Cook the potatoes in a saucepan of boiling water for 15-20 minutes, or until tender. Drain and, using a potato masher, crush into small pieces. Place in a large bowl.

2. Place the nuts and onion in a food processor or blender and, using the pulse button, chop finely. Add the nuts, onion, apple, cheese and breadcrumbs to the potatoes in the bowl. Season to taste with salt and pepper. Mix well, then shape into four to six equal-sized patties. Coat in the flour, then cover and leave to chill in the refrigerator for 1 hour.

3. Preheat the barbecue. Brush the burgers with the oil and cook over medium coals for 5-6 minutes on each side, or until cooked through.

4. Place the lettuce leaves on the bottom halves of the buns and top with the burgers. Top with red onion slices, add the lids and serve immediately.

BLUE CHEESE CAN BE A DOMINEERING FLAVOUR, BUT NOT WHEN MIXED WITH APPLES AND NUTS IN A BURGER LIKE THIS. SINCE THEY ARE ALL FRIDGE AND STORECUPBOARD INGREDIENTS YOU CAN MAKE THIS RECIPE AT ANY TIME.

TURKEY & TARRAGON BURGERS

PREP TIME: 20 minutes, plus chilling   **COOK TIME: 20-30 minutes**

WHAT A HEALTHY COMBINATION OF INGREDIENTS THERE IS IN THESE BURGERS. TURKEY AND TARRAGON CONTRIBUTE FINE, DISTINCTIVE FLAVOURS, WHILE THE ROBUST BULGAR WHEAT IS THERE FOR ITS NUTTY TASTE AND COARSE TEXTURE.

MAKES 4

55 g/2 oz bulgar wheat
450 g/1 lb fresh turkey mince
1 tbsp finely grated orange rind
1 red onion, finely chopped
1 yellow pepper, deseeded, peeled and finely chopped
25 g/1 oz toasted flaked almonds
1 tbsp chopped fresh tarragon
1-2 tbsp sunflower oil
salt and pepper
lettuce leaves
tomato relish
tomato and onion salad, to serve

1. Cook the bulgar wheat in a saucepan of lightly salted boiling water for 10-15 minutes, or according to the packet instructions.

2. Drain the bulgar wheat and place in a bowl with the turkey mince, orange rind, onion, yellow pepper, almonds, tarragon and salt and pepper to taste. Mix together, then shape into four equal-sized burgers. Cover and leave to chill in the refrigerator for 1 hour.

3. Preheat the barbecue. Brush the burgers with the oil and cook over medium-hot coals for 5-6 minutes on each side, or until cooked through.

4. Put a few lettuce leaves on serving plates and place a burger on top of each, spoon over a little relish and serve immediately with a tomato and onion salad.

STEP 1

STEP 2

STEP 3

TARRAGON HAS A SLIGHT TASTE OF ANISEED (ALSO KNOWN AS ANISE) AND IS THE PERFECT PARTNER TO TURKEY, CHICKEN AND FISH.

SWEET POTATO & HALLOUMI BURGERS

PREP TIME: 10-12 minutes, plus chilling   **COOK TIME: 40-45 minutes**

MAKES 4—6

450 g/1 lb sweet potatoes, cut into chunks

175 g/6 oz broccoli florets

2-3 garlic cloves, crushed

1 red onion, finely chopped or grated

1½-2 fresh red jalapeño chillies, deseeded and finely chopped

175 g/6 oz halloumi cheese, grated

2 tbsp wholemeal flour

2-3 tbsp sunflower oil

450 g/1 lb onions, sliced

1 tbsp chopped fresh coriander

salt and pepper

1. Cook the sweet potato in a saucepan of lightly salted boiling water for 15-20 minutes, or until tender. Drain and mash. Cut the broccoli into small pieces, cook in a separate saucepan of boiling water for 3 minutes, then drain and plunge into cold water. Drain again, then add to the mashed sweet potato.

2. Stir in the garlic, onion, chilli, cheese and salt and pepper to taste. Mix well and shape into four to six equal-sized patties, then coat in the flour. Cover and leave to chill in the refrigerator for at least 1 hour.

3. Heat 1½ tablespoons of the oil in a heavy-based frying pan. Add the onions and fry over a medium heat for 12-15 minutes, or until softened. Stir in the coriander and reserve.

4. Preheat the barbecue. Brush the patties with the remaining oil and cook over medium coals for 5-6 minutes on each side, or until cooked through.

5. Top the burgers with the reserved fried onions and coriander and serve immediately.

STEP 1

STEP 2

STEP 2

THERE ARE LOTS OF
INTERESTING TEXTURES AND
FLAVOURS VYING FOR YOUR
ATTENTION IN THESE TASTY
BURGERS. FOR AN EXTRA CHEESY
KICK, SHALLOW-FRY SOME SLICES
OF HALLOUMI CHEESE TO SERVE
ON TOP OF THE BURGERS.

BURGERS TARTARE

PREP TIME: *20 minutes*   COOK TIME: *10 minutes*

DON'T WORRY, THESE AREN'T ACTUALLY RAW BURGERS.
RATHER, THEY USE THE TRADITIONAL ACCOMPANIMENTS
FOR STEAK TARTARE TO CREATE A REMARKABLY
JUICY BURGER.

MAKES 6

6 gherkins
2 tbsp capers
1 tsp pickled green
   peppercorns
2 egg yolks
1 tsp salt
675 g/1 lb 8 oz fresh
   lean beef mince
6 burger buns, split
6 tbsp mayonnaise

1. Preheat the grill to high. Place the rack 5–8 cm/2–3¼ inches below the heat.

2. Meanwhile, finely chop the gherkins, capers and peppercorns.

3. Put the egg yolks into a large bowl and lightly beat. Stir in the gherkins, capers, peppercorns and salt. Add the beef and gently but thoroughly work in the egg mixture. Divide into six equal-sized portions and shape each portion into a patty.

4. Lay the patties on a large baking sheet, place on the grill rack and cook under the preheated grill for about 4 minutes until they are sizzling and starting to brown. Turn and cook on the other side for about 4 minutes, or until the burgers are cooked to your liking.

5. Meanwhile, spread each bun with about 1 tablespoon of the mayonnaise. Place the burgers in the buns and serve immediately.

STEP 5

STEP 2

ADD A FEW DASHES OF
TABASCO SAUCE FOR THOSE
WHO LIKE THEIR FOOD SPICY.

SALMON BURGERS WITH PINE NUTS

PREP TIME: **15 minutes, plus chilling**   *COOK TIME:* **25–35 minutes**

MAKES 4–6

300 g/10½ oz potatoes, peeled and cut into chunks

450 g/1 lb fresh salmon fillet, skinned

175 g/6 oz spinach leaves

55 g/2 oz pine nuts, toasted

2 tbsp finely grated lemon rind

1 tbsp chopped fresh parsley

2 tbsp wholemeal flour

200 ml/7 fl oz crème fraîche

4-cm/1½-inch piece cucumber, peeled and finely chopped

2 tbsp sunflower oil

salt and pepper

4–6 wholemeal buns, split

grilled cherry tomatoes, to serve

1. Cook the potatoes in a saucepan of lightly salted boiling water for 15–20 minutes, or until tender. Drain well, then mash and reserve. Chop the salmon into chunks.

2. Reserve a few spinach leaves for serving, then blanch the remainder in a saucepan of boiling water for 2 minutes. Drain, squeezing out any excess moisture, then chop.

3. Place the spinach in a food processor or blender with the salmon, potatoes, pine nuts, 1 tablespoon of the lemon rind, the parsley and salt and pepper to taste and, using the pulse button, blend together. Shape into four to six equal-sized burgers, then cover and leave to chill in the refrigerator for 1 hour. Coat the burgers in the flour.

4. Mix the crème fraîche, cucumber and the remaining lemon rind together in a bowl, then cover and leave to chill until required.

5. Preheat the barbecue. Brush the burgers with the oil and cook over medium-hot coals for 4–6 minutes on each side, or until cooked through.

6. Place the reserved spinach leaves on the bottom halves of the buns and top with the burgers, then spoon over a little of the crème fraîche mixture. Add the lids and serve immediately with grilled cherry tomatoes.

FRESH SALMON, SPINACH AND
PINE NUTS CREATE A VERY
COLOURFUL BURGER. BE SURE
TO SQUEEZE AS MUCH WATER
AS POSSIBLE OUT OF THE FRESH
SPINACH, OTHERWISE THE
BURGERS MAY BE RATHER SOGGY.

LEMON & MINT TURKEY BURGERS

PREP TIME: 10 minutes, plus chilling

COOK TIME: 15 minutes

MAKES 12

500 g/1 lb 2 oz fresh turkey mince

½ small onion, grated

finely grated rind and juice of 1 small lemon

1 garlic clove, finely chopped

2 tbsp finely chopped fresh mint

½ tsp pepper

1 tsp sea salt

1 egg, beaten

1 tbsp olive oil

lemon wedges, to serve

1. Place all the ingredients except the oil in a bowl and mix well with a fork. Divide into 12 equal-sized portions and shape each portion into a patty. Cover and chill in the refrigerator for at least 1 hour, or overnight.

2. Heat the oil in a large heavy-based frying pan. When the oil starts to look hazy add the burgers, cooking in batches if necessary. Cook over a medium-high heat for 4–5 minutes on each side, until golden brown and cooked through.

3. Transfer the burgers to a warmed serving plate and serve immediately with the lemon wedges for squeezing over.

TURKEY MEAT IS LEANER THAN CHICKEN AND GREAT FOR THOSE WHO ARE CONSCIOUS OF THEIR FAT AND CALORIE INTAKE. SERVE WITHOUT BREAD AND WITH ROASTED VEGETABLES, INSTEAD OF CHIPS, FOR AN ULTRA-HEALTHY BURGER MEAL.

PASTRAMI BURGERS

PREP TIME: *15 minutes*   **COOK TIME:** *10 minutes*

THE ORIGINS OF THESE OVER-THE-TOP BURGERS IS UNCLEAR, BUT SOMEHOW THEY HAVE TAKEN ROOT IN SALT LAKE CITY, UTAH.

MAKES 4

450 g/1 lb fresh beef mince
1 tsp salt
½ tsp pepper
1 tbsp butter
Gruyère cheese slices
4 sesame seed burger buns, split
50 ml/2 fl oz shop-bought Thousand Island dressing
shredded lettuce leaves
225 g/8 oz sliced pastrami

1. Place the mince into a medium-sized bowl with the salt and pepper and mix gently to combine. Divide into four equal-sized portions and shape each portion into a patty.

2 Heat a ridged griddle pan or large frying pan over a medium-high heat. Add the butter and heat until it has stopped foaming. Add the patties and cook for about 4 minutes, without moving, until they are brown and release easily from the pan. Turn and cook on the other side for 2 minutes, then put a slice of cheese on top of each burger and cook for a further 3 minutes, or until cooked to your liking.

3. Place the open buns on plates. Spread with the Thousand Island dressing, then place some shredded lettuce on each bun base. Set a burger on top, then pile with the pastrami. Serve immediately.

STEP 1

STEP 2

STEP 2

COMBINE THIS DELICIOUS BURGER WITH SOME HOME-MADE MUSTARD (SEE PAGE 174), OR FOR AN ADDED KICK, SOME HOME-MADE CHIPOTLE MUSTARD (SEE PAGE 180).

CRAB BURGERS

PREP TIME: *25 minutes, plus chilling*   **COOK TIME:** *less than 15 minutes*

IN MARYLAND, EXTRA-LARGE CRAB CAKE SANDWICHES ARE OFTEN SERVED IN BUNS WITH LETTUCE AND TOMATOES, JUST LIKE BURGERS.

MAKES 6

450 g/1 lb crabmeat
150 ml/5 fl oz mayonnaise
1 tbsp chopped fresh parsley
1 tsp Old Bay seasoning or other seafood seasoning mix
1 egg
1 tsp Worcestershire sauce
1 tsp mustard powder
½ tsp salt
¼ tsp pepper
30 g/1 oz dried breadcrumbs
2 tbsp butter
6 burger buns, split
tomato slices
shredded lettuce leaves
Tartare Sauce (see page 182) and lemon wedges, to serve

1. Place the crabmeat into a medium-sized bowl and add the mayonnaise, parsley, Old Bay seasoning, egg, Worcestershire sauce, mustard, salt and pepper. Gently mix, then add the breadcrumbs, a little at a time, and mix very gently until combined. Chill in the refrigerator for at least 30 minutes.

2. Divide the mixture into six equal-sized portions and shape each portion into a patty.

3. Heat a ridged griddle pan over a medium heat, add the butter and heat until no longer foaming, stirring to coat the base of the pan. Add the patties and cook for about 6-7 minutes on each side until golden.

4. Put the burgers in the buns and top with the tomato slices, lettuce and tartare sauce. Serve immediately with lemon wedges.

YOU CAN BUY OLD BAY SEASONING FROM SPECIALTY STORES OR MAKE YOUR OWN BY GRINDING AND COMBINING 1 TABLESPOON EACH OF CELERY SEED, WHOLE BLACK PEPPERCORNS AND SWEET PAPRIKA, HALF A TEASPOON EACH OF WHOLE CARDAMOM AND MUSTARD SEEDS, QUARTER OF A TEASPOON OF MACE, 4 WHOLE CLOVES AND 6 BAY LEAVES.

91

STEAKHOUSE BURGERS

PREP TIME: *20 minutes, plus chilling*   **COOK TIME:** *10 minutes*

THE VERY BEST BURGERS ARE MADE WITH FRESHLY CHOPPED MEAT, AND YOU DON'T NEED A MEAT GRINDER FOR THE TASK.

MAKES 4

450 g/1 lb boneless braising steak or a mixture with at least 20 per cent fat
1 tsp salt
½ tsp pepper
4 burger buns, split
Gruyère cheese slices
2 tbsp mayonnaise
2 tbsp tomato ketchup
lettuce leaves
tomato slices

1. Preheat the barbecue to medium-high. Chop the beef into 2.5-cm/1-inch cubes, then place on a plate, wrap in clingfilm and chill in the refrigerator for about 30 minutes.

2. Place half the beef in a food processor or blender. Pulse (do not run the processor) about 15 times. Season the meat with half the salt and half the pepper, and pulse a further 10–15 times until the meat is finely chopped but not over-processed. Remove from the processor and repeat with the remaining beef. Divide into four equal-sized portions and shape each portion into a patty.

3. Place the patties on the rack and cook until brown and cooked to your liking, 3 minutes on each side for medium rare and 4 minutes on each side for medium. Place a slice of cheese on each burger during the last 2 minutes of cooking.

4. Meanwhile, put the mayonnaise and ketchup into a small bowl and mix to combine. Spread on the buns, then add the burgers with the lettuce leaves and tomato slices. Serve immediately.

KA-POW!

SMOKED BURGERS

PREP TIME: 25 minutes   **COOK TIME:** 10 minutes

SLICED ONIONS, COOKED SLOWLY UNTIL GOLDEN BROWN AND SLIGHTLY SWEET, ARE A DELICIOUS ACCOMPANIMENT TO ALL KINDS OF BURGERS.

MAKES 4

wood chips, for smoking

450 g/1 lb fresh beef mince
1 tsp salt
½ tsp pepper
smoked Gouda cheese slices
4 brioche buns, split

FIG RELISH

1 quantity Caramelized Onions (see page 202)
75 g/2¾ oz fig jam
1 tbsp red wine vinegar
1 tbsp soy sauce
1 tsp Worcestershire sauce
pepper

1. Soak the wood chips in water for at least 10 minutes.

2. To make the relish, put the caramelized onions, jam, vinegar, soy sauce, Worcestershire sauce and pepper to taste into a medium-sized saucepan. Bring to a low simmer and cook for 1–2 minutes, until it forms a thick relish. Set aside.

3. Place the mince in a bowl with the salt and pepper and gently mix to combine. Divide into four equal-sized portions and shape each portion into a patty.

4. If using a gas barbecue, wrap the drained wood chips in foil, making a pouch but leaving the ends open to allow the smoke to escape. Lift the grate, place the pouch on top of a side burner, and turn the heat to high. Turn the other burners to medium or low, cover and preheat the barbecue to 200°C/400°F.

5. If using a charcoal barbecue, preheat to medium-high. Push the coals to one side and place the wood chips on top.

6. When the wood starts smoking, put the burgers on the rack on the opposite side of the barbecue. Cover and cook for about 4 minutes until brown, then turn and cook on the other side. After 2 minutes, add the cheese and cook for a further 2 minutes, or until the burgers are brown and cooked to your liking.

7. Place the burgers in the buns and top with some of the relish. Serve immediately.

STEP 6

STEP 3

SMOKED GOUDA CHEESE ADDS EXTRA SMOKY FLAVOUR TO THIS LIGHTLY SMOKED HAMBURGER, AND A SWEET-SOUR FIG SAUCE IS A DELICIOUS ACCOMPANIMENT.

BLT BURGERS WITH ASPARAGUS

PREP TIME: 12 minutes, plus chilling   COOK TIME: 15 minutes

MAKES 4-6

225 g/8 oz back bacon rashers

450 g/1 lb fresh steak mince

1 onion, grated

2-4 garlic cloves, crushed

1-2 tbsp sunflower oil

salt and pepper

lettuce leaves

4-6 burger buns, split

tomato slices

DIP

175 g/6 oz baby asparagus spears

1 tbsp lemon juice

1 small ripe avocado, peeled, stoned and finely chopped

2 firm tomatoes, peeled, deseeded and finely chopped

150 ml/5 fl oz crème fraîche

salt and pepper

1. Remove any rind and fat from the bacon rashers and chop finely.

2. Place the bacon, steak mince, onion, garlic and salt and pepper to taste in a large bowl and mix well. Shape into four to six equal-sized patties, then cover and leave to chill in the refrigerator for 30 minutes.

3. To make the dip, trim the asparagus and cook in a saucepan of lightly salted boiling water for 5 minutes, then drain and plunge into cold water. When cold, drain and finely chop half the spears into a bowl and reserve the rest to serve. Sprinkle the lemon juice over the avocado. Stir in the avocado, tomatoes and crème fraîche. Add salt and pepper to taste, cover and leave to chill in the refrigerator until required.

4. Preheat the barbecue. Lightly brush the burgers with the oil and cook over hot coals for 3-4 minutes on each side, or until cooked to your liking.

5. Place the lettuce leaves on the bottom halves of the buns and top with the burgers. Top with a tomato slice, an asparagus spear and a spoonful of the dip. Add the lids and serve immediately.

WHAT COULD BE BETTER FOR FANS OF THE BLT THAN A BLT BURGER? THE ASPARAGUS AND AVOCADO DIP ADDS THAT EXTRA TASTE DIMENSION. WHEN MAKING DIPS OR SALSAS, PREPARE THEM AT LEAST 30 MINUTES BEFORE USING TO ALLOW TIME FOR THE FLAVOURS TO DEVELOP.

BURGERS WITH SAUTÉED MUSHROOMS

PREP TIME: 25 minutes   **COOK TIME:** 25 minutes

THE ADDITION OF SAUTÉED DICED MUSHROOMS ADDS A NOTE OF COMPLEXITY TO THE BEEF IN THESE LUSCIOUS BURGERS.

MAKES 4

1 tbsp extra virgin olive oil, plus extra for frying

1 garlic clove, finely chopped

½ tsp finely chopped fresh rosemary or thyme

225 g/8 oz mushrooms, stalks removed, very finely chopped

450 g/1 lb fresh beef mince

mature Cheddar cheese slices

½ tsp salt

¼ tsp pepper

4 brioche buns, split

softened butter, for spreading

salt and pepper

1. Heat the oil in a large frying pan over a medium heat. Add the garlic and rosemary and sauté for 30 seconds until fragrant. Add the mushrooms and stir for 1 minute until well coated. Season to taste with salt and pepper, then reduce the heat slightly and cook for a further 15 minutes, stirring frequently, until the liquid evaporates and the mushrooms are very tender and dry.

2. Place the mushrooms in a medium-sized bowl and leave to cool, then add the beef and ½ teaspoon of salt and ¼ teaspoon of pepper. Stir gently, then divide into 4 equal-sized portions and shape each portion into a patty.

3. Return the pan to a medium-high heat. Add enough oil to coat the base of the pan. Add the patties and cook for about 4 minutes until they are brown and release easily from the pan. Turn and cook for 2 minutes, then place a slice of cheese on top of each patty and cook for a further 2 minutes, or until cooked to your liking.

4. Spread the butter on the buns, add the burgers and bun lids and serve immediately.

STEP 1

STEP 2

STEP 3

THIS SAUTÉED MUSHROOM MIXTURE IS COMMONLY KNOWN AS DUXELLES AND USED MOST NOTABLY IN BEEF WELLINGTON. ADD SHALLOTS FOR A MORE AUTHENTIC FLAVOUR AND CREAM FOR A MORE LUXURIOUS VERSION.

TRUFFLE BURGERS

PREP TIME: *10 minutes*   **COOK TIME:** *20 minutes*

THESE BURGERS ARE TOPPED WITH TRUFFLE OIL AND A PARMESAN CRISP AND ARE SERVED OPEN-FACED ON A PIECE OF FOCACCIA.

MAKES 4

450 g/1 lb fresh sirloin steak mince or other premium beef mince

175 g/6 oz freshly grated Parmesan cheese

½ tsp salt

½ tsp pepper

4 x 15-cm/6-inch square pieces of focaccia

1 tsp white truffle oil

1. Preheat the grill to high. In a large bowl, gently combine the beef, 55 g/2 oz of the cheese and the salt and pepper. Divide the mixture into four equal-sized portions and shape each portion into a patty. Place the patties on a baking sheet and set aside.

2. Heat a small, non-stick frying pan over a medium heat. Pile a quarter of the remaining cheese into two small rounds, spaced well apart, and heat until melted. Using a slotted spoon, transfer the rounds to a plate to cool and harden. Repeat with the remaining cheese to make four rounds in total.

3. Place the patties under the preheated grill and cook for about 4 minutes until sizzling and turning brown on top. Turn and cook for a further 4 minutes until brown and cooked to your liking.

4. Place each burger on a piece of focaccia and drizzle each with a ¼ teaspoon of the oil. Top with a Parmesan crisp and serve immediately.

PARMESAN CRISPS CAN ALSO BE MADE IN THE OVEN ON A NON-STICK BAKING TRAY, OR EVEN IN THE MICROWAVE. JUST ENSURE THAT THE CHEESE ISN'T PILED TOO HIGH AND THAT THERE'S PLENTY OF ROOM FOR THE MELTED CHEESE TO SPREAD.

POLENTA COD BURGERS

PREP TIME: 15 minutes, plus cooling and chilling   **COOK TIME:** 18-20 minutes

PERKED UP WITH BASIL AND FRESH PARMESAN, THESE COD BURGERS ARE FANTASTICALLY TASTY. THE POLENTA THAT HOLDS ALL THE INGREDIENTS TOGETHER IS VERY EASY TO PREPARE.

MAKES 4–6

300 ml/10 fl oz water

225 g/8 oz instant polenta

450 g/1 lb cod fillets, skinned

1 tbsp chopped fresh basil

55 g/2 oz Parmesan cheese, grated

2 tbsp plain flour

1–2 tbsp olive oil

salt and pepper

4–6 wedges of ciabatta bread

Aioli (see page 192)

baby spinach leaves and roasted Mediterranean vegetables, to serve

1. Place the water in a large saucepan and bring to the boil. Slowly pour in the polenta in a steady stream and cook over a gentle heat, stirring constantly, for 5 minutes or until thick. Leave to cool for about 10 minutes.

2. Place the polenta, fish, basil, cheese and salt and pepper to taste in a food processor or blender and, using the pulse button, blend together. Shape into four to six equal-sized burgers, then coat in the flour. Cover and leave to chill in the refrigerator for 1 hour.

3. Preheat the barbecue. Brush the burgers with the oil and cook over medium-hot coals for 4-5 minutes on each side, or until cooked through.

4. Place each burger onto a ciabatta wedge and top with a spoonful of aioli. Serve immediately with baby spinach leaves and roasted Mediterranean vegetables.

COD CONTAINS A GOOD AMOUNT OF VITAMIN A, WHICH HELPS TO HEAL THE GUT LINING, A VERY IMPORTANT PART OF ADDRESSING FOOD INTOLERANCES.

TURKEY GORGONZOLA BURGERS

PREP TIME: *10 minutes*   **COOK TIME:** *10 minutes*

LEAVE BLAND TURKEY BURGERS BEHIND WITH THESE
BURGERS FILLED WITH BLUE CHEESE AND BLACK PEPPER.
THEY ARE MOIST AND FLAVOURSOME ENOUGH
TO STAND ON THEIR OWN.

MAKES 4

2 shallots, finely chopped
½ tsp salt
½ tsp pepper
55 g/2 oz Gorgonzola or other blue cheese, crumbled
450 g/1 lb fresh turkey mince
4 crusty bread rolls, split

1. Preheat the barbecue to medium-high. Put the shallots, salt, pepper and cheese into a bowl and combine. Add the turkey and gently break up the mince while working all the ingredients together.

2. Divide the mixture into four equal-sized portions and shape each portion into a patty.

3. Place the patties on the rack and cook for about 4 minutes on each side until brown and cooked through. Place the burgers in the buns and serve immediately.

PORCINI MUSHROOM BURGERS

PREP TIME: 10 minutes   **COOK TIME:** less than 10 minutes

DRIED PORCINI MUSHROOMS GROUND TO A POWDER DELICATELY PERFUME AND SEASON THE BEEF IN THESE BURGERS.

MAKES 4

½ cup dried porcini mushrooms

2 tbsp olive oil, plus extra for greasing

1 tsp salt

½ tsp pepper

450 g/1 lb fresh beef mince

55 g/2 oz grated Gruyère cheese

4 brioche buns, split

4 tsp softened butter

Caramelized Onions (see page 202)

1. Grind the mushrooms to a powder in a spice grinder or clean coffee grinder. You should have about 2 tablespoons. Put the powder into a bowl with the oil, salt and pepper and stir until the salt is dissolved. If necessary, add up to 2 teaspoons of water to thin the mixture. Add the beef and gently mix to combine, then divide into four equal-sized portions and form each portion into a patty.

2. Heat a griddle pan over medium-high heat, then coat with oil. Put the patties in the pan and cover. Cook for about 4 minutes on each side until browned. After 2 minutes, put the cheese on top of the burgers and cook for an additional 2 minutes until the burgers are browned and cooked to your liking.

3. Spread the buns with butter, and place the burgers in the buns. Top with the onions and serve immediately.

SMOKED SALT BURGERS

PREP TIME: *30 minutes*   **COOK TIME:** *20 minutes*

FLAVOURED SALTS ARE A GREAT WAY TO ADD QUICK AND EASY FLAVOUR TO BURGERS. HERE SMOKED SALT ADDS A LIGHTLY SMOKED FLAVOUR TO OPEN-FACED BURGERS TOPPED WITH BRIGHT CHARGRILLED SUMMER VEGETABLES.

MAKES 6

2 small courgettes
2 tomatoes
6 thick slices sourdough bread
2 tbsp olive oil, plus 1 tbsp for drizzling
675 g/1 lb 8 oz fresh beef mince
1½ tsp smoked salt, plus extra to taste

1. Preheat the barbecue to high. Cut the ends and two sides off the courgettes, then cut lengthways into 1-cm/½-inch slices. You will need a total of 12 long, thin slices.

2. Cut the tops and bottoms off the tomatoes, then thickly slice crossways.

3. Brush the courgettes, tomatoes and bread with the oil.

4. Combine the mince and the smoked salt in a bowl. Divide into six equal-sized portions and shape each portion into a patty.

5. Put the vegetables and bread on the rack. Cook for about 3 minutes on each side until grill marks appear and the courgettes are tender. Remove from the heat and season to taste with smoked salt.

6. Put the patties on the rack and cook for 4 minutes on each side. Place each burger on a piece of the grilled bread and season to taste with smoked salt. Top each burger with two courgette slices and one to two tomato slices. Drizzle with oil and serve immediately.

SMOKED SALT CAN BE BOUGHT IN ALL GOOD SUPERMARKETS BUT IT'S ALSO SURPRISINGLY EASY TO MAKE YOUR OWN. THERE ARE BARBECUE, STOVE-TOP, GRILL AND EVEN WOK METHODS.

BLUE CHEESE-STUFFED BURGERS

PREP TIME: 20 minutes   *COOK TIME: 10 minutes*

INSTEAD OF RAW ONIONS, THESE OOZING-WITH-CHEESE BURGERS ARE ALSO DELICIOUS TOPPED WITH SWEET-SOUR FIG RELISH (SEE PAGE 94).

MAKES 4

550 g/1 lb 4 oz fresh beef mince
1 tsp salt
½ tsp pepper
55-85 g/2-3 oz blue cheese, cut into 4 chunks
vegetable oil, for frying
4 brioche buns, split
lettuce leaves
tomato slices
red onion slices

1. Place the mince into a medium-sized bowl with the salt and pepper and gently mix to combine. Divide into four equal-sized portions and roll each portion into a ball. Use your finger to make a hole in each ball, then stuff a chunk of cheese inside. Press to seal the outside and flatten into 1-cm/½-inch thick patties.

2. Place a large, non-stick frying pan or ridged griddle pan over a medium-high heat. Add enough vegetable oil to just cover the base, then add the patties and cook for 4-5 minutes on each side until brown and cooked through (some cheese may escape).

3. Put the burgers in the buns, top with the lettuce leaves, tomato and onion and serve immediately.

STEP 2

STEP 3

THIS IS A PARTICULARLY IMPRESSIVE BURGER — AND CERTAINLY ONE FOR BLUE CHEESE-LOVERS. MAKE THIS RECIPE TO IMPRESS YOUR GUESTS AT A SUMMER BARBECUE, OR EVEN A DINNER PARTY.

FOUR-PEPPER VEAL BURGERS

PREP TIME: 25 minutes   COOK TIME: 20 minutes

THESE BURGERS HIGHLIGHT THE TENDER TEXTURE OF VEAL
MINCE WITH A HIT OF FOUR-COLOUR PEPPERCORNS.
LIGHTLY FRIED SHALLOTS AND PEPPERY ROCKET
MAKE THESE BURGERS SPECIAL.

MAKES 4

3 shallots
2 tbsp olive oil
450 g/1 lb fresh veal mince
1 tsp salt
½ tsp mixed ground black, white, green and pink peppercorns
4 x 15-cm/6-inch square pieces of focaccia, split
large handful of rocket leaves

1. Peel and thinly slice the shallots, then separate the rings. Heat the oil in a large frying pan over a high heat until shimmering and add the shallot rings. They should sizzle immediately. Cook for about 10 minutes, stirring occasionally, until well browned. Use a slotted spoon or tongs to remove the shallots from the oil and drain on layers of kitchen paper. Set the pan aside.

2. Put the mince into a large bowl and sprinkle over the salt and peppercorns. Gently break up the meat and toss with the seasoning until well combined. Divide into four equal-sized portions and shape each portion into a patty.

3. Pour most of the oil out of the pan and return the pan to the stove. Heat to a medium-high heat, add the patties and cook for about 4 minutes on each side until brown and cooked to your liking.

4. Place each burger on a piece of focaccia and top with the fried shallots, rocket and the remaining pieces of focaccia. Serve immediately.

STEP 3

STEP 1

EAL MINCE CAN SOMETIMES BE DIFFICULT TO FIND IN THE SUPERMARKET. IF THIS IS THE CASE, YOU CAN SUBSTITUTE WITH CHICKEN, TURKEY OR EVEN LAMB.

PORTOBELLO MUSHROOM BURGERS WITH MOZZARELLA

PREP TIME: 10 minutes   COOK TIME: 15 minutes

THIS VEGETARIAN BURGER COMBINES MARINATED
PORTOBELLO MUSHROOMS WITH MOZZARELLA
CHEESE AND PESTO IN A FOCACCIA 'BUN'.

MAKES 4

4 tsp olive oil

2 tsp red wine vinegar

1 garlic clove, finely chopped

4 large Portobello mushrooms, caps only

4–8 slices fresh vegetarian mozzarella-style cheese

4 x 15-cm/6-inch square pieces focaccia, split

50 ml/2 fl oz pesto

tomato slices

baby rocket leaves

salt and pepper

1. Preheat the grill to high and the oven to 160°C/325°F/Gas Mark 3. Whisk together the oil, vinegar and garlic in a medium-sized bowl. Place the mushrooms gill side-up on a baking tray, then drizzle with the vinaigrette and season to taste with salt and pepper.

2. Place under the preheated grill and cook for about 5–8 minutes until the mushrooms are tender. Place the cheese slices on top and cook for a further 1–2 minutes until bubbling. Meanwhile, put the focaccia on a lower rack in the preheated oven for 5 minutes to warm through.

3. Lightly spread the focaccia with the pesto, then add the mushrooms. Top with the tomato slices and rocket and serve immediately.

SLIDERS

PREP TIME: 15 minutes   COOK TIME: 7 minutes

SLIDERS ARE MINI BURGERS THAT MAY HAVE BEEN NAMED FOR THE WAY THEY SLID AROUND WHEN SERVED IN THE GALLEYS OF TOSSING AND TURNING US NAVY SHIPS AT SEA.

MAKES 12

450 g/1 lb fresh beef mince

1 tsp salt

½ tsp pepper

1–2 tsp butter

85 g/3 oz Cheddar cheese, sliced and cut into 5-cm/2-inch squares

12 mini burger buns or small bread rolls, split

1. Place the beef in a medium-sized bowl, add the salt and pepper, then divide into 12 equal-sized portions and shape each portion into a patty.

2. Heat a griddle pan over a medium–high heat. Add enough butter to lightly coat the pan, using a spatula to spread it over the base. Add the patties and cook for 3 minutes on one side until brown, then turn and add the cheese. Cook for a further 2–3 minutes, or until brown and cooked to your liking.

3. Place the burgers in the buns and serve immediately.

KA-BOOM!!

STEP 1

STEP 2

STEP 2

These small burgers are perfect for entertaining. For large crowds, make the patties with different meats to provide your guests with a variation of tastes and textures.

119

JAMAICAN JERK CHICKEN BURGERS

PREP TIME: 25 minutes   **COOK TIME:** 20 minutes

CHICKEN MINCE IS SPICED UP WITH JAMAICAN JERK SEASONING FOR THESE DELICIOUS BURGERS.

MAKES 4

1 tsp soft light brown sugar

1 tsp ground ginger

½ tsp ground allspice

½ tsp dried thyme

½–1 tsp cayenne pepper or chopped fresh jalapeño chilli

1 tbsp lime juice

2 garlic cloves, finely chopped

½ tsp salt

½ tsp pepper

450 g/1 lb fresh chicken mince

1 tbsp vegetable oil

1 red pepper or yellow pepper, deseeded and cut into large flat pieces

1 tsp olive oil

1 tsp red wine vinegar

4 onion rolls, split

lettuce leaves

salt and pepper

1. Place the sugar, ginger, allspice, thyme, cayenne pepper, lime juice, garlic, the salt and pepper into a bowl and mix together. Add the chicken and gently mix to combine. Divide the mixture into four equal-sized portions and shape each portion into a patty.

2. Place a griddle pan over a medium-high heat and add the vegetable oil. Add the red pepper and cook for about 5 minutes, turning frequently, until blackened. Transfer to a bowl, cover with clingfilm or a plate and leave to steam for 5 minutes. Remove the skin and cut the flesh into strips. Toss with the olive oil, vinegar, and salt and pepper to taste.

3. Put the patties in the pan and cook, covered, for about 5 minutes on each side until brown and cooked through. Place the burgers in the rolls and top with the lettuce and peppers. Serve immediately.

LONDON BURGERS

FEEL FREE TO COOK THE EGGS TO YOUR LIKING, BUT NOTE THAT A BIT OF A RUNNY YOLK MAKES A LOVELY SAUCE ON THESE BURGERS.

MAKES 4

450 g/1 lb fresh beef mince
2 tbsp Worcestershire sauce
4 English muffins
4 tbsp butter
2 tsp vegetable oil
4 eggs
½ tsp salt
½ tsp pepper

1. Combine the mince with half the Worcestershire sauce in a large bowl. Divide the mixture into four equal-sized portions and shape each portion into a patty about 1 cm/½ inch wider than the muffins, making a dimple in the centre of each patty.

2. Split the muffins and spread each half with butter.

3. Heat a large frying pan over a medium-high heat. Place the muffin halves in the pan buttered side down and cook for about 2 minutes. Put two muffin halves on each of four plates.

4. Add the patties to the pan and cook for about 4 minutes until brown. Turn and cook on the other side for 4 minutes, or until cooked to your liking. Place a burger on one of the muffin halves on each plate and drizzle with the remaining Worcestershire sauce.

5. Add the oil to the pan, swirling to coat. Add the eggs and sprinkle with the salt and pepper. Cover and cook for about 3 minutes until the whites are set and the yolks are beginning to set at the edges. Top each burger with an egg and the top half of a muffin. Serve immediately.

THESE BURGERS WOULD
MAKE THE PERFECT BREAKFAST
TREAT. WHY NOT ADD SOME
CRISPY BACON AND HOME-MADE
TOMATO KETCHUP (SEE PAGE
170) FOR ADDED INDULGENCE.

MOROCCAN LAMB BURGERS

PREP TIME: 20 minutes, **COOK TIME:** 12 minutes
plus standing

MAKES 4

550 g/1 lb 4 oz fresh
lamb mince
1 onion, grated
1 tsp harissa sauce
1 garlic clove, crushed
2 tbsp finely chopped
fresh mint
½ tsp cumin seeds,
crushed
½ tsp paprika
oil, for greasing
salt and pepper
4 pitta breads, warmed
and split
red onion slices
shredded lettuce leaves

YOGURT & CUCUMBER SAUCE

½ large cucumber
4 tbsp natural yogurt
6 tbsp chopped fresh
mint
salt

1. To make the sauce, peel the cucumber, quarter lengthways and scoop out the seeds. Chop the flesh and put in a sieve set over a bowl. Sprinkle with salt, cover with a plate and weigh down with a can of vegetables. Leave to drain for 30 minutes, then mix with the remaining ingredients.

2. Combine the lamb, onion, harissa sauce, garlic, mint, cumin seeds and paprika. Season to taste with salt and pepper, mixing well with a fork. Divide into four equal-sized portions and flatten into patties about 2.5 cm/1 inch thick. Cover and leave to stand at room temperature for 30 minutes.

3. Preheat the barbecue. Lightly brush the burgers with oil. Grease the grill rack. Cook over hot coals for 5–6 minutes on each side, or until cooked through.

4. Stuff the burgers into warmed pitta breads with the red onion, lettuce leaves and a spoonful of the sauce. Serve immediately.

AUSSIE BURGERS

PREP TIME: *20 minutes*   **COOK TIME:** *less than 12 minutes*

AUSTRALIANS LOVE TO PUT BEETROOT ON THEIR BURGERS. GRILLED PINEAPPLE AND FRIED EGGS ARE OTHER AUSSIE ADD-ONS THAT MAKE THIS MILE-HIGH BURGER EXTRA SATISFYING.

MAKES 4

450 g/1 lb fresh beef mince

1 tsp salt

½ tsp pepper

4 slices canned pineapple

2–3 tsp vegetable oil, for brushing and frying

4 eggs

mayonnaise, for spreading

4 soft burger buns, split

4–8 slices beetroot in vinegar

lettuce leaves

tomato slices

salt and pepper

1. Place the beef in a medium-sized bowl with 1 teaspoon of salt and ½ teaspoon of pepper. Mix gently to combine, then divide into four equal-sized portions and shape each portion into a patty.

2. Place a griddle pan over a medium-high heat and add 1 teaspoon of the oil. Lightly brush the pineapple with oil and place the patties and pineapple in the pan. Cover and cook the pineapple for 3 minutes on each side until it is soft and marked, and cook the burgers for about 4 minutes on each side until brown and cooked to your liking. Remove from the heat and keep warm.

3. Add enough oil to a frying pan to lightly cover the base, swirling to coat the pan. Add the eggs and season to taste with salt and pepper. Cover and cook for about 3 minutes until the whites are set and the yolks are beginning to set at the edges.

4. Spread some mayonnaise on each half of the buns. Place a pineapple slice on each bun base, then add a burger, egg, one to two beetroot slices, a lettuce leaf and a tomato slice. Finish with the bun tops and serve immediately.

STEP 2

STEP 3

STEP 4

OTHER TRADITIONAL ACCOMPANIMENTS TO THIS MONUMENTAL BURGER INCLUDE BACON AND CHEESE. ALL YOU NEED TO DO NEXT IS WORK OUT HOW TO ATTACK IT!

BARBECUED CAJUN PORK BURGERS

PREP TIME: *20 minutes, plus chilling*   **COOK TIME:** *35-45 minutes*

MAKES 4—6

225 g/8 oz sweet potatoes, cut into chunks

450 g/1 lb fresh pork mince

1 eating apple, peeled, cored and grated

2 tsp Cajun seasoning

450 g/1 lb onions

1 tbsp chopped fresh coriander

2 tbsp sunflower oil

8-12 lean back bacon rashers

salt and pepper

1. Cook the sweet potato in a saucepan of lightly salted boiling water for 15-20 minutes, or until soft when pierced with a fork. Drain well, then mash and reserve.

2. Place the pork in a bowl, add the mashed potato, apple and Cajun seasoning. Grate one of the onions and add to the pork mixture with the coriander and salt and pepper to taste. Mix together, then shape into four to six equal-sized patties. Cover and leave to chill in the refrigerator for 1 hour.

3. Slice the remaining onions. Heat 1 tablespoon of the oil in a frying pan. Add the onions and cook over a low heat for 10-12 minutes, stirring until soft. Remove the frying pan from the heat and reserve. Wrap each patty in two bacon rashers.

4. Preheat the barbecue. Cook the patties over hot coals, brushing with the remaining oil, for 4-5 minutes on each side, or until thoroughly cooked. Alternatively, cook in a ridged griddle pan or under a hot grill. Serve immediately with the fried onions.

THE CAJUN SEASONING REALLY LIVENS UP THE FLAVOUR OF THESE PORK BURGERS. YOU SHOULD KEEP THIS SEASONING IN A COOL, DARK PLACE. IF EXPOSED TO HEAT OR LIGHT, ITS PUNGENCY QUICKLY DISAPPEARS.

THAI CRAB BURGERS WITH BEANSPROUTS

PREP TIME: 10 minutes, plus chilling   **COOK TIME:** 10 minutes

MAKES 4

1½ tbsp sunflower oil

1 fresh red chilli, deseeded and finely chopped

2.5-cm/1-inch piece fresh root ginger, grated

2 lemon grass stalks, outer leaves removed and finely chopped

350 g/12 oz canned white crabmeat, drained and flaked

225 g/8 oz cooked peeled prawns, thawed if frozen and squeezed dry

175 g/6 oz cooked Thai rice

1 tbsp chopped fresh coriander

115 g/4 oz beansprouts

6 spring onions, finely chopped

1 tbsp soy sauce

1–2 tbsp wholemeal flour

1. Heat a wok or frying pan and when hot add 2 teaspoons of the oil, the chilli, ginger and lemon grass and stir-fry over medium-high heat for 1 minute. Remove the wok from the heat and leave to cool.

2. Place the chilli mixture, crabmeat, prawns, rice, chopped coriander, beansprouts, spring onions and soy sauce in a food processor or blender and, using the pulse button, blend together. Shape into four equal-sized patties, then coat in the flour. Cover and leave to chill in the refrigerator for 1 hour.

3. Heat a heavy-based, non-stick frying pan and add the remaining oil. When hot, add the patties and cook over a medium heat for 3–4 minutes on each side or until piping hot. Serve immediately.

STEP 1

STEP 2

STEP 2

CRABMEAT IS A GREAT SOURCE OF PROTEIN AND IS ALSO LOW IN FAT AND HAS FEW CALORIES. SERVE THIS DELICIOUS BURGER WITH TARTARE SAUCE (SEE PAGE 182).

HAWAIIAN BURGERS WITH CHARGRILLED PINEAPPLE

PREP TIME: 25 minutes   **COOK TIME: 10 minutes**

THE FLAVOURS OF THE HAWAIIAN ISLANDS COME INTO PLAY IN THIS PORK BURGER SERVED WITH CHARGRILLED PINEAPPLE.

MAKES 4

450 g/1 lb fresh pork mince

3 tbsp teriyaki sauce, plus extra for spreading

4 slices canned pineapple

onion slices

vegetable oil, for brushing

4 Hawaiian rolls, or other sweet rolls, split

lettuce leaves

1. Preheat the barbecue to medium-high. Place the mince into a medium-sized bowl and season with the teriyaki sauce, mixing gently until incorporated. Divide into four equal-sized portions and form each portion into a patty.

2. Lightly brush the pineapple and onion with oil. Place the patties, onion and pineapple on the rack and cover. Cook the onion and pineapple for 3-4 minutes on each side until soft and marked. Cook the burgers for 4 minutes on each side until brown and cooked through.

3. Spread both halves of the buns with teriyaki sauce. Put the burgers in the buns with the pineapple, onion and lettuce and serve immediately.

MEXICAN TURKEY BURGERS

PREP TIME: *10 minutes, plus chilling* **COOK TIME:** *10-12 minutes*

MAKES 4

450 g/1 lb fresh turkey mince

200 g/7 oz canned refried beans

2-4 garlic cloves, crushed

1-2 fresh jalapeño chillies, deseeded and finely chopped

2 tbsp tomato purée

1 tbsp chopped fresh coriander

1 tbsp sunflower oil

salt and pepper

shredded baby spinach leaves

4 cheese-topped burger buns, split

salsa

Guacamole (see page 186)

tortilla chips, to serve

1. Place the turkey mince in a bowl and break up any large lumps. Beat the refried beans until smooth, then add to the turkey in the bowl.

2. Add the garlic, chillies, tomato purée and coriander with salt and pepper to taste and mix together. Shape into four equal-sized patties, then cover and leave to chill in the refrigerator for 1 hour.

3. Preheat the barbecue. Brush the patties with the oil and cook over medium-hot coals for 5-6 minutes on each side, or until cooked through.

4. Place the spinach on the bottom halves of the burger buns and top with the burgers. Spoon over a little salsa and guacamole and top with the lids. Serve immediately with tortilla chips on the side.

THERE ARE MANY VARIETIES OF FRESH CHILLIES AVAILABLE. IF YOU ARE IN DOUBT AS TO THE CHILLI'S HEAT, THEN START WITH THE MILDER CHILLIES, SUCH AS JALAPEÑO, AND GRADUALLY MOVE ON TO THE HOTTER ONES.

ARGENTINE BURGERS WITH CHIMICHURRI

PREP TIME: 25 minutes, plus chilling   **COOK TIME:** less than 15 minutes

USING FRESH MINCE ADDS AN EXTRA BEEFY FLAVOUR TO THESE BURGERS INSPIRED BY THE BARBECUED STEAKS AND TANGY CHIMICHURRI SAUCE OF ARGENTINA.

MAKES 4

450 g/1 lb fresh boneless braising steak with at least 20 per cent fat

40 g/1½ oz onion, finely chopped

2 tbsp fresh lemon juice

2 tbsp finely chopped fresh parsley

2 tbsp finely chopped fresh mint

1 garlic clove, finely chopped

1 tsp red pepper flakes or chilli flakes

50 ml/2 fl oz olive oil

4 French rolls, split

avocado slices

salt and pepper

1. Preheat the barbecue to medium-high. Cut the beef into 2.5-cm/1-inch cubes, then place on a plate, wrap in clingfilm and chill in the refrigerator for about 30 minutes until very cold.

2. Meanwhile, combine the onion, lemon juice, parsley, mint, garlic, chilli flakes, and salt and pepper to taste in a small bowl. Stir in the oil and set aside.

3. Place half the beef in a food processor or blender and pulse about 15 times. Season to taste with salt and pepper and pulse a further 10 to 15 times until the meat is finely chopped but not over processed. Remove from the processor and repeat with the remaining meat.

4. Divide the meat into four equal-sized portions and shape each portion into a patty.

5. Place the patties on the rack and cook for 3 minutes on each side for medium rare, and 4 minutes on each side for medium.

6. Place the burgers in the rolls. Top with the avocado slices and a few spoonfuls of the sauce. Serve immediately.

STEP 2

STEP 3

STEP 6

CHIMICHURRI IS TRADITIONALLY SERVED WITH STEAK, HENCE THE BRAISING STEAK USED IN THIS RECIPE. IT IS ALSO DELICIOUS SERVED WITH CHICKEN OR FISH.

BENTO BURGERS

PREP TIME: *15 minutes, plus resting*   **COOK TIME:** *15 minutes*

THESE JAPANESE VEGAN SNACKS ARE MADE WITH COOKED RICE PRESSED INTO THE SHAPE OF BUNS, CRISP ON THE OUTSIDE, WITH SAVOURY SPINACH INSIDE.

MAKES 5

8 shiitake mushrooms, stalks removed

450 g/1 lb washed spinach leaves

2 tbsp soy sauce

2 tbsp mirin

2 tsp sesame seeds, toasted

1 tsp salt

225 ml/8 fl oz lukewarm water

425 g/15 oz short- or medium-grain white rice, rinsed and cooked and kept warm

2 tsp sesame oil, for frying

1. Preheat the grill to high. Arrange the mushrooms on the grill pan and cook for 3 minutes on each side until brown and tender. Thinly slice the mushrooms and place in a medium-sized bowl.

2. Bring a large saucepan of water to the boil. Add the spinach and blanch for 1 minute. Drain, cool under cold running water, then squeeze dry. Add the mushrooms to the spinach, then add the soy sauce, mirin and sesame seeds and combine.

3. Dissolve the salt in the warm water. Place the rice in a wide bowl and divide into ten equal-sized portions. Wet your hands with the water and very firmly press each portion into a rice bun. Wet your hands each time you make a bun. Leave to set for 20 minutes.

4. Place a non-stick frying pan or ridged griddle pan over a medium heat and lightly coat the base with oil. Add the rice buns and cook for 4 minutes on each side (turning very gently) until brown.

5. Put the spinach mixture on top of half the rice buns, then top with the remaining buns. Wrap the burgers in squares of baking paper to hold them together prior to serving and serve within 2 hours.

STEP 3

STEP 1

RINSING THE RICE HELPS IT
STICK TOGETHER, AND USING
SHORT- OR MEDIUM-GRAIN
RICE IS ESSENTIAL.

KIMCHI BURGERS

PREP TIME: *20 minutes, plus chilling*   **COOK TIME:** *20 minutes*

THE BRIGHT, SPICY TASTE OF KOREAN KIMCHI
(SPICY FERMENTED CABBAGE) IS HIGHLIGHTED
WITH SAUTÉED SPRING ONIONS AND GINGER
IN THESE JUICY BURGERS.

MAKES 6

450 g/1 lb fresh beef mince

225 g/8 oz fresh pork mince

1 tbsp finely grated fresh ginger

1 tsp soy sauce

10 spring onions

1 tsp vegetable oil

6 sesame seed buns, split

225 ml/8 fl oz kimchi

1. Preheat the barbecue to high. Put the beef, pork, ginger and soy sauce into a large bowl and mix to combine. Finely chop two spring onions and mix them into the meat. Divide the meat into six equal-sized portions and shape each portion into a patty. Cover and chill in the refrigerator.

2. Meanwhile, cut the remaining spring onions into 10-cm/4-inch lengths and brush them with oil. Place on the rack and cook for about 5 minutes, turning, until tender and brown. Set aside.

3. Place the patties on the rack and cook for about 4 minutes on each side until they are marked and cooked through.

4. Put the burgers in the buns and top with the spring onions and some kimchi. Serve immediately.

KA-POW!

YOU CAN BUY KIMCHI FROM
SPECIALIST ASIAN STORES, OR
EVEN MAKE YOUR OWN AT HOME.
THERE ARE MANY VARIATIONS,
SO YOU CAN DECIDE UPON THE
RECIPE THAT BEST SUITS YOUR
TASTES OR MOOD.

GREEN CHILLI CHEESEBURGERS

PREP TIME: *25 minutes*   **COOK TIME:** *20 minutes*

IT'S EASY ENOUGH TO THROW SOME ROASTED GREEN CHILLIES AND A BIT OF CHEESE ON A BURGER, BUT THIS RECIPE WORKS THOSE FLAVOURS INTO THE MEAT FOR A SUPREMELY MOIST BURGER WITH A SOUTHWESTERN FLAIR.

MAKES 6

3 large mild green chillies

675 g/1 lb 8 oz fresh lean beef mince

1 tsp salt

115 g/4 oz Cheddar cheese, grated, plus 6 thin slices

6 soft burger buns, split

1. Preheat the barbecue to high. Place the chillies on the rack and cook, turning frequently, until black all over. Wrap them in foil and leave to stand for 15 minutes. Peel off the skins, remove the stems and finely chop.

2. Put the mince, salt, chopped chillies and grated cheese into a large bowl and gently mix to combine.

3. Divide the mixture into six equal-sized portions and form each portion into a patty. Place the patties on the rack and cook for 4 minutes. Turn, top each burger with a slice of cheese, then cover and cook for a further 4 minutes until cooked to your liking and the cheese is melted. Place the burgers in the buns and serve immediately.

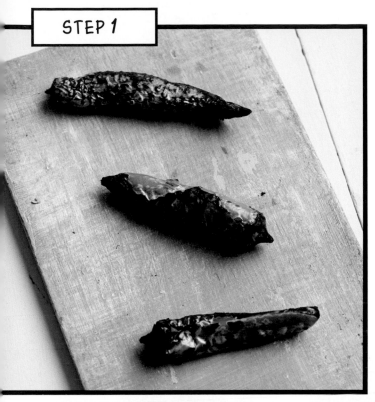

STEP 1

STEP 2

STEP 3

THIS RECIPE USES LARGE MILD CHILLIES BUT IF YOU PREFER A HOTTER BURGER, JUST REPLACE WITH SOME FIERY BIRD'S EYE CHILLIES INSTEAD.

LAMB-CUMIN PITTA BURGERS WITH TAHINI SAUCE

PREP TIME: *25 minutes*

COOK TIME: *less than 15 minutes*

THESE PITTA BURGERS ARE A LITTLE SMALLER THAN THE AVERAGE BURGER, BUT THE RICH LAMB PATTIES TOPPED WITH FRESH VEGETABLES AND TAHINI SAUCE ARE VERY FILLING.

MAKES 6

450 g/1 lb fresh lamb mince

3 tbsp finely chopped red onion

1 tbsp chopped fresh coriander, plus extra leaves to garnish

1 tsp salt

½ tsp pepper

½ tsp ground cumin

90 ml/3 fl oz tahini

90 ml/3 fl oz natural yogurt

1 garlic clove, finely chopped

3 large pitta breads, warmed, halved and split

tomato slices

cucumber slices

olive oil, for drizzling

salt and pepper

1. Preheat the grill to high, place the lamb in a medium-sized bowl and add the onion, coriander, 1 teaspoon of salt, ½ teaspoon of pepper and the cumin, then gently mix to combine. Divide into six equal-sized portions, form each portion into a 7.5-cm/3-inch wide patty and place in a grill pan lined with foil.

2. Place the pan under the preheated grill and cook the patties for about 5-7 minutes on each side, or until cooked through and brown.

3. Put the tahini, yogurt and garlic into a bowl, season to taste with salt and pepper and mix to combine. Stuff the burgers into the pitta halves, then drizzle with the tahini sauce. Add the tomato and cucumber slices and the coriander leaves, drizzle with the oil and serve immediately.

144

TAHINI, OR SESAME SEED PASTE, MAKES A VERSATILE ADDITION TO THE KITCHEN CUPBOARD. THE DARKER VERSION IS PREFERABLE AS IT DOESN'T HAVE THE NUTRITIOUS OUTER HULL REMOVED, BUT IT CAN BE A LITTLE RICH FOR SOME TASTES.

145

KHEEMA BURGERS WITH RAITA

PREP TIME: 30 minutes   COOK TIME: 15 minutes

LIKE AN INDIAN RAITA, YOGURT SAUCE AND WILTED CUCUMBERS COOL OFF THE SPICE IN THESE DELICIOUS BURGERS.

MAKES 6

2 tbsp vegetable oil

1 onion, chopped

450 g/1 lb fresh lean beef mince

5-cm/2-inch piece fresh ginger, finely chopped

2 garlic cloves, finely chopped

1 tsp ground coriander

1 tsp ground cumin

1 tsp salt

½ tsp turmeric

½ tsp cayenne pepper

½ tsp ground nutmeg

6 thin flatbreads

YOGURT SAUCE

1 small garlic clove, finely chopped

½ tsp garam masala

½ tsp salt

1 tsp lemon juice

225 ml/8 fl oz Greek-style yogurt

CUCUMBERS

1 small cucumber

½ tsp salt

2 tsp lemon juice

1. Add 1 tablespoon of the oil to a large frying pan over a high heat. Add the onion and cook for about 10 minutes, stirring frequently, until beginning to brown. Remove from the pan and set aside, leaving any remaining oil in the pan.

2. Meanwhile, to make the sauce, stir the garlic, garam masala, salt and lemon juice into the yogurt. Set aside to develop the flavours. To prepare the cucumbers, halve lengthways, deseed and finely chop the cucumber, then toss with the salt and lemon juice. Set aside to develop the flavours.

3. Place the beef into a large bowl with the onion, ginger, garlic, coriander, cumin, salt, turmeric, cayenne pepper and nutmeg and mix to combine. Divide into six equal-sized portions and shape each portion into a 15-cm/6-inch long oval patty.

4. Return the pan to a high heat and add the remaining oil. Add the patties and cook on one side for about 5 minutes until brown. Turn and cook on the other side for about 5 minutes until cooked to your liking.

5. Set each burger on a piece of flatbread, top with 1 tablespoon of the yogurt sauce and a portion of cucumbers. Roll the sides of the flatbread to encase the filling. Serve immediately with any remaining yogurt sauce and cucumbers.

STEP 1

STEP 5

THERE ARE MANY VARIATIONS OF RAITA – FROM THE CLASSIC CUCUMBER, AS USED HERE, TO MINT AND AUBERGINE. THE VARIETIES ARE ENDLESS!

SPICED LENTIL-POTATO BURGERS

PREP TIME: *30 minutes*   **COOK TIME:** *45 minutes*

WHOLESOME AND VEGETARIAN, THESE BURGER PATTIES ARE
MADE WITH LENTILS SIMMERED IN INDIAN SPICES
AND BOUND WITH MASHED POTATO.

MAKES 6

100 g/3½ oz green lentils

1 carrot, peeled and diced

2 tbsp vegetable oil, plus extra for frying

1 tbsp brown mustard seeds

1 tsp ground coriander

1 tsp ground cumin

40 g/1½ oz onion, finely chopped

1 tsp finely chopped garlic

1 fresh serrano chilli, finely chopped, or ½ tsp cayenne pepper

55 g/2 oz frozen peas, thawed

1 potato, cooked, peeled and mashed

55 g/2 oz fresh breadcrumbs

6 wholemeal buns, split

ready-made coriander chutney or mango chutney

lettuce leaves

salt and pepper

1. Bring a large saucepan of lightly salted water to the boil. Add the lentils, bring back to the boil, then reduce the heat and simmer for 15 minutes. Add the carrot and cook for about 10 minutes until the lentils are quite soft. Drain.

2. Heat the oil in a medium-sized sauté pan. Add the mustard seeds, coriander and cumin and swirl to coat in the oil. Add the onion, garlic and chilli and cook for 5–8 minutes, stirring frequently, until the onion is soft. Stir in the lentils and carrot and simmer for about 5 minutes to evaporate any liquid. Add the peas and potato and season to taste with salt and pepper, then combine thoroughly.

3. Place the breadcrumbs in a shallow bowl. Scoop out the lentil mixture in six equal-sized portions and shape each portion into a patty. Press each patty in the breadcrumbs to cover both sides.

4. Place a griddle pan or large frying pan over a medium heat and add enough oil to coat the base. Add the patties and cook for about 5 minutes on each side until brown.

5. Place the burgers in the buns, top with the chutney and lettuce leaves, and serve immediately.

WITH *26* PER CENT OF THEIR CALORIFIC VALUE COMING FROM PROTEIN, LENTILS ARE AN IMPORTANT STAPLE IN ANY DIET, CREATING STRONG SKIN, NAILS AND HAIR.

LOCO MOCO

THIS CROSS-CULTURAL HAWAIIAN SPECIALTY OF ASIAN RICE TOPPED WITH A BURGER AND A FRIED EGG, ALL SMOTHERED WITH GRAVY, IS OFTEN ENJOYED AS A POST-SURF BREAKFAST.

MAKES 4

300 g/10½ oz medium-grain rice

1 tbsp butter, plus extra for griddling

1 tbsp flour

450 ml/16 fl oz beef broth

450 g/1 lb fresh beef mince

4 eggs

salt and pepper

1. Cook the rice according to the packet instructions. Keep warm.

2. Melt the butter in a medium-sized frying pan over a medium-low heat. Whisk in the flour, then cook, stirring, for 4 minutes until lightly browned. Whisk in the broth, bring to simmering point and simmer for 20 minutes until thickened. Season to taste with salt and pepper and keep warm.

3. Meanwhile, place the beef into a medium-sized bowl and lightly season with salt and pepper, then divide into four equal-sized portions and form each portion into a patty.

4. Add enough butter to a frying pan to coat the base of the pan and melt over a medium-high heat. Add the patties to the pan and cook for 4 minutes on each side, or until cooked to your liking. Remove from the pan and keep warm.

5. Add the eggs to the pan and sprinkle with salt and pepper. Cook for about 3–4 minutes until the whites are set and the yolks are beginning to set at the edges.

6. Divide the rice between four plates and top each portion with a burger, an egg and lots of gravy. Serve immediately.

STEP 1

STEP 2

STEP 5

THIS IS CERTAINLY A DIFFERENT BURGER DISH TO TRY AND BECAUSE OF ITS UNUSUAL COMBINATION OF INGREDIENTS YOU CAN TUCK IN FOR BREAKFAST, LUNCH OR DINNER.

CHILLI-GARLIC SAUCE BURGER

PREP TIME: *20 minutes, plus chilling*   **COOK TIME:** *20 minutes*

A MIXTURE OF BEEF AND PORK HELP MAKE THESE SPICY BURGERS DISTINCTIVE AND DELICIOUS.

MAKES 4

large bunch fresh coriander
1 garlic clove
225 g/8 oz fresh beef mince
225 g/8 oz fresh pork mince
2 tbsp red chilli sauce
2 tsp finely grated ginger
2 tsp soy sauce
2 small pak choi
2 tsp vegetable oil
4 burger buns, split

1. Finely chop half of the coriander leaves. Finely chop the garlic.

2. Place the beef, pork, chilli sauce, ginger, soy sauce, garlic and chopped coriander into a large bowl and mix to combine. Divide the mixture into four equal-sized portions and shape each portion into a 1–2-cm/^{1}/$_2$–^{3}/$_4$-inch thick patty. Cover and chill in the refrigerator.

3. Rougly chop the pak choi, discarding the thick ends. Heat a large frying pan over a high heat and add the oil, swirling to cover the base of the pan. Add the pak choi and cook, stirring frequently, until wilted. Set aside.

4. Place the patties in the pan and cook for about 4 minutes until brown. Turn and cook for a further 4 minutes until they are cooked through and brown on both sides.

5. Place the burgers in the buns. Top each burger with some sautéed pak choi and the remaining whole coriander leaves. Serve immediately.

THIS IS THE PERFECT BURGER FOR CHILLI-LOVERS EVERYWHERE. JUST REDUCE THE AMOUNT OF CHILLI SAUCE USED IF YOU PREFER A MILDER TASTE.

163

BURGERS WITH SESAME & PONZU MAYO

PREP TIME: 20 minutes   **COOK TIME: 10 minutes**

A COMBINATION OF YUZU (A JAPANESE CITRUS FRUIT), BONITO FLAKES, SEAWEED, MIRIN AND SOY SAUCE, PONZU SAUCE HAS ALL THE RIGHT FLAVOURS ROLLED INTO ONE BOTTLE TO GARNISH THESE DELICIOUS, JUICY BURGERS.

MAKES 4

450 g/1 lb fresh turkey mince

2 tbsp sesame seeds

4 tsp soy sauce, plus extra to serve

1 tsp toasted sesame oil

1 tsp finely chopped garlic

4 tbsp mayonnaise

2 tbsp ponzu sauce

4 sesame burger buns, split

25 g/1 oz baby lettuce leaves

tomato slices

pepper

1. Place the turkey into a medium-sized bowl with the sesame seeds, soy sauce, oil, garlic, and pepper to taste and gently mix to combine. Divide into four equal-sized portions and form each portion into a patty. Place the patties on a large baking sheet.

2. Preheat the grill to high and place the rack below the heat. Place the patties on the rack and grill for 5 minutes, then turn and continue cooking for a further 4–5 minutes until cooked through.

3. Combine the mayonnaise and ponzu sauce in a small bowl (the mixture will be thin). Coat each cut side of the buns with the sauce, then add the burgers. Top with some lettuce leaves and tomato slices, then sprinkle with pepper and a drizzle of soy sauce. Serve immediately.

165

BEEF TERIYAKI BURGERS WITH SIZZLING VEGETABLES

PREP TIME: 10 minutes, plus chilling   **COOK TIME:** 10–15 minutes

MAKES 4

450 g/1 lb steak mince

8 spring onions

2–4 garlic cloves

2.5-cm/1-inch piece fresh ginger, grated

½ tsp wasabi or freshly grated horseradish, or to taste

3 tsp teriyaki sauce or marinade

2 tsp peanut oil

115 g/4 oz carrot, grated

115 g/4 oz pak choi, shredded

55 g/2 oz cucumber, shredded

4 burger buns, split

crispy fried seaweed, to garnish (optional)

1. Place the steak mince, spring onions, garlic, ginger, wasabi and the teriyaki sauce in a food processor or blender and, using the pulse button, blend together. Shape into four equal-sized patties, then cover and leave to chill in the refrigerator for 30 minutes.

2. Heat a heavy-based frying pan and add 1 teaspoon of the oil. When hot, add the patties and cook over a medium heat for 3–5 minutes on each side or until cooked to your liking. Add more oil if necessary. Keep warm.

3. Spoon a little of the vegetables onto the bun bases and top with the burgers and seaweed, if using. Add the bun lids and serve immediately.

A BLEND OF SOY SAUCE, WINE, VINEGAR, VARIOUS SPICES AND A HINT OF SWEETNESS, TERIYAKI SAUCE IS USED AS A MARINADE TO TENDERIZE THE BEEF AND INFUSE IT WITH SOME ORIENTAL FLAVOURS.

CHAPTER 4
THE AWESOME SIDE-SHOW

HOME-MADE TOMATO KETCHUP

PREP TIME: 10 minutes   **COOK TIME:** 15-20 minutes

TOMATO KETCHUP IS A HUGELY POPULAR STORECUPBOARD STAPLE AND MANY PEOPLE NEVER THINK TO MAKE THEIR OWN. THIS RECIPE IS SURPRISINGLY QUICK AND EASY AND TASTES UTTERLY SUPERB.

MAKES ABOUT 250 ML/ 9 FL OZ

2 tbsp olive oil

1 red onion, peeled and chopped

2 garlic cloves, chopped

250 g/9 oz plum tomatoes, chopped

250 g/9 oz canned chopped tomatoes

½ tsp ground ginger

½ tsp chilli powder

40 g/1½ oz dark brown sugar

100 ml/3½ fl oz red wine vinegar

salt and pepper

1. Heat the olive oil in a large saucepan and add the onion, garlic and all the tomatoes. Add the ginger and chilli and season with salt and pepper to taste. Cook for 15 minutes, or until soft.

2. Pour the mixture into a food processor or blender and blend well. Sieve thoroughly to remove all the seeds. Return the mixture to the pan and add the sugar and vinegar. Return to the boil and cook until it is the consistency of ketchup.

3. Bottle quickly in sterilized bottles or jars and store in a cool place or refrigerator until required.

STEP 1

STEP 2

TO STERILIZE JARS, MAKE SURE THEY ARE WASHED IN HOT SOAPY WATER AND RINSED WELL, THEN HEAT IN A MODERATE OVEN FOR 5 MINUTES.

BARBECUE SAUCE

PREP TIME: *15 minutes*   **COOK TIME:** *20 minutes*

MAKES ABOUT 225 ML/ 8 FL OZ

1 tbsp olive oil

1 small onion, finely chopped

2-3 garlic cloves, crushed

1 fresh red jalapeño chilli, deseeded and finely chopped (optional)

2 tsp tomato purée

1 tsp (or to taste) dry mustard

1 tbsp red wine vinegar

1 tbsp Worcestershire sauce

2-3 tsp muscovado sugar

300 ml/10 fl oz water

1. Heat the oil in a small heavy-based saucepan, add the onion, garlic and chilli, if using, and gently sauté, stirring frequently, for 3 minutes, or until beginning to soften. Remove from the heat.

2. Blend the tomato purée with the mustard, the vinegar and the Worcestershire sauce to a paste, then stir into the onion mixture with 2 teaspoons of the sugar. Mix well, then gradually stir in the water.

3. Return to the heat and bring to the boil, stirring frequently. Reduce the heat and gently simmer, stirring occasionally, for 15 minutes. Taste and add the remaining sugar, if liked. Strain, if preferred, and serve hot or leave to cool and serve cold.

BARBECUE SAUCE IS THE ULTIMATE BURGER ACCOMPANIMENT AND TURNS THE AVERAGE BURGER INTO SOMETHING EXTRA SPECIAL.

HOME-MADE MUSTARD

PREP TIME: *15 minutes plus developing*   **COOK TIME:** *no cooking*

LIKE A SPICY COUNTRY-STYLE DIJON MUSTARD, THIS MUSTARD IS EASY TO MAKE BUT TAKES A FEW DAYS TO FINISH. THE FLAVOUR IMPROVES AND BECOMES LESS SPICY AFTER A COUPLE OF DAYS IN THE REFRIGERATOR.

MAKES 175 ML/6 FL OZ

3 tbsp brown mustard seeds
3 tbsp apple cider vinegar
1-2 tbsp water
3 tbsp mustard powder
2 tsp salt
2 tsp honey

1. Put the mustard seeds into a small, non-metallic container with the vinegar and enough water to cover completely. Set aside for two days, covered, at room temperature.

2. Strain the mustard seeds, reserving the liquid. Grind in a spice grinder until some seeds are still whole while some are ground. You may have to push the seeds down and grind again, but the more you grind, the spicier the mustard will be.

3. Place the mixture in a small bowl with the mustard powder, salt and honey. Add the reserved vinegar water and stir.

4. Place in a sterilized jar, seal and refrigerate for at least 2 days before serving.

COLESLAW

PREP TIME: *10 minutes, plus chilling*   COOK TIME: *no cooking*

COLESLAW IS A SUMMER PARTY STAPLE. IT WORKS PERFECTLY AS PART OF A SALAD, A BURGER TOPPING, OR SIMPLY ON ITS OWN.

SERVES 10–12

150 ml/5 fl oz mayonnaise

150 ml/5 fl oz natural yogurt

dash of Tabasco sauce

1 head of white cabbage

4 carrots

1 green pepper

salt and pepper

1. To make the dressing, mix the mayonnaise, yogurt, Tabasco sauce and salt and pepper to taste together in a small bowl. Chill in the refrigerator until required.

2. Cut the cabbage in half and then into quarters. Remove and discard the tough centre stalk. Finely shred the cabbage leaves. Wash the leaves under cold running water and dry thoroughly on kitchen paper. Peel the carrots and roughly grate or shred in a food processor or on a mandoline. Quarter and deseed the pepper and cut the flesh into thin strips.

3. Mix the vegetables together in a large serving bowl and toss to mix. Pour over the dressing and toss until the vegetables are well coated. Cover and chill in the refrigerator until required.

There are many great add-ons to this popular dish. You can try nuts, seeds, apple, raisins and capers. Cheese also adds a great twist.

HOME-MADE PICKLE RELISH

PREP TIME: *15 minutes, plus chilling*   **COOK TIME:** *20 minutes*

THIS RELISH LIGHTLY PICKLES THE CUCUMBERS AS PART OF THE PROCESS OF MAKING THE RELISH, GIVING IT A BRIGHT, FRESH FLAVOUR.

MAKES 950 G/ 2 LB 2 OZ

4 cucumbers

350 ml/12 fl oz cider vinegar

1 tsp mustard seeds

1 tsp coriander seeds

50 g/1¾ oz sugar

2 tsp salt

1 green pepper deseeded and chopped

1 small white onion, chopped

1. Top and tail the cucumbers, cut them in half lengthways, deseed and finely chop.

2. Bring the vinegar to the boil in a large saucepan. Add the cucumbers and cook for about 4 minutes, stirring frequently until they are just starting to lose their colour and are tender but still crunchy.

3. Use a slotted spoon to scoop the cucumbers out of the vinegar and set them aside. Add the mustard seeds and coriander seeds to the vinegar and bring back to the boil. Stir in the sugar and salt and reduce the heat to simmering. Cook until the vinegar mixture is reduced to 125 ml/4 fl oz.

4. Mix together the green pepper and onion with the cooked cucumber. Pour the vinegar over the vegetables and stir to combine. Transfer the relish to sterilized jars. Cover and chill in the refrigerator for at least 1 hour before serving.

STEP 4

STEP 1

THIS RELISH PROVIDES A GREAT BITE TO ANY BURGER. IT WILL KEEP IN THE REFRIGERATOR FOR UP TO 1 MONTH.

CHIPOTLE KETCHUP & CHIPOTLE MUSTARD

KETCHUP PREP TIME: 5 minutes
MUSTARD PREP TIME: under 5 minutes

KETCHUP COOK TIME: 8-10 minut
MUSTARD COOK TIME: no cooking

WHY NOT ADD AN EXTRA-SPECIAL SPICY KICK TO YOUR FAVOURITE BURGER TOPPINGS? THESE RECIPES ARE SO EASY BUT ARE SURE TO ALWAYS IMPRESS.

MAKES 225 ML/8 FL OZ

CHIPOTLE KETCHUP

225 ml/8 fl oz prepared ketchup

½ tsp Worcestershire sauce

½ tsp light brown sugar

1 tbsp fresh lemon juice, or to taste

1½ tsp chipotle powder, or to taste

1 tsp ground cumin

½ tsp ground turmeric

¼ tsp ground ginger

salt

CHIPOTLE MUSTARD

½ cup Dijon mustard

1 tsp chipotle powder, or to taste

1. For the ketchup, combine all the ingredients with salt to taste in a small saucepan and place over a medium heat. Bring to a simmer and cook, stirring frequently, for 5 minutes, or until the ketchup is slightly thickened. Remove from the heat and cool. Transfer to a sterilized jar, cover, and refrigerate until ready to use.

2. To make the chipotle mustard, place the ingredients in a small bowl and stir to thoroughly combine. Transfer to a sterilized jar, cover, and refrigerate until ready to use.

180

CHIPOTLE IS A DRIED, SMOKED JALAPEÑO – IT IS USED FREQUENTLY IN MEXICAN COOKING AND ADDS A GREAT, DISTINCTIVE SMOKY FLAVOUR TO ANY DISH.

TARTARE SAUCE

PREP TIME: 10 minutes, plus chilling   COOK TIME: no cooking

TARTARE SAUCE IS DELICIOUS ON ALMOST ANY
SEAFOOD-BASED BURGER, INCLUDING THE ORIGINAL FISH
BURGER (SEE PAGE 58).

MAKES ABOUT 225 ML/ 8 FL OZ

2 small gherkins
1 spring onion
1 tbsp capers
handful of fresh
flat-leaf parsley
175 ml/6 fl oz
mayonnaise
1 tbsp lemon juice
salt and pepper

1. Finely chop the gherkins, spring onion, capers and parsley. Put them into a small bowl and stir in the mayonnaise.

2. Add the lemon juice and stir, then season to taste with salt and pepper. Cover and chill in the refrigerator for at least 30 minutes or up to 2 days before serving.

FOR A MORE UNUSUAL TWIST
TO THIS CLASSIC FISH SAUCE,
ADD EITHER SOME CHOPPED
HARD-BOILED EGGS OR
OLIVES — OR BOTH!

TOMATO & RED ONION RELISH

PREP TIME: 15 minutes

COOK TIME: 1 hour 25 minutes–1 hour 40 minutes

SERVES 4

OVEN-DRIED TOMATOES

8 ripe tomatoes
1–2 tbsp virgin olive oil
salt and pepper

SAUCE

1 tbsp virgin olive oil
2 large red onions, thinly sliced
55 g/2 oz rocket or baby spinach leaves

1. For the oven-dried tomatoes, preheat the oven to 150°C/300°F/ Gas Mark 2. Cut the tomatoes in half, and arrange all the halves in a large roasting tin. Drizzle with the oil and season to taste with salt and pepper. Cook in the oven for 1¼–1½ hours, or until roasted but still moist.

2. For the sauce, heat the oil in a large frying pan. Add the onions and fry over a gentle heat until soft and golden brown. Place eight of the oven-dried tomatoes in a food processor or blender and process until puréed. Add to the onions in the frying pan.

3. Slice the remaining eight tomato halves and add to the frying pan with the rocket. Season to taste with salt and pepper and cook until the leaves have just wilted. Serve immediately.

STEP 1

STEP 2

STEP 3

THIS RECIPE IS PERFECT IF YOU GROW YOUR OWN TOMATOES. WHETHER THEY'RE FROM YOUR GARDEN OR SHOP-BOUGHT, MAKE SURE THEY'RE THE RIPEST YOU CAN FIND.

GUACAMOLE

PREP TIME: *15 minutes, plus chilling*

COOK TIME: *no cooking*

SERVES 4

1 ripe tomato

2 limes

2-3 ripe small to medium avocados, or 1-2 large ones

1/4- 1/2 onion, finely chopped

pinch of ground cumin

pinch of mild chilli powder

1/2-1 fresh green chilli, such as jalapeño or serrano, deseeded and finely chopped

1 tbsp finely chopped fresh coriander leaves, plus extra to garnish

1. Place the tomato in a heatproof bowl, pour over boiling water to cover and leave for 30 seconds. Drain and plunge into cold water. Peel off the skin. Cut the tomato in half, deseed and chop the flesh.

2. Squeeze the juice from the limes into a small bowl. Cut 1 avocado in half around the stone. Twist the two halves apart in opposite directions, then remove the stone with a knife. Carefully peel off the skin, dice the flesh and toss in the bowl of lime juice to prevent the flesh discolouring. Repeat with the remaining avocados. Mash the avocados coarsely with a fork.

3. Add the onion, tomato, cumin, chilli powder, chilli and coriander to the avocados and mix together. Chill, covered, in the refrigerator until ready to serve.

KA-POW!

A GOOD GUACAMOLE ALWAYS DEPENDS ON USING QUALITY, RIPE AVOCADOS. MASHING RATHER THAN PURÉEING GIVES CONTROL OVER THE TEXTURE.

187

MAYONNAISE

PREP TIME: 5 minutes **COOK TIME:** no cooking

ONE OF THE BASIC SAUCES IN THE FRENCH REPERTOIRE, HOME-MADE MAYONNAISE HAS A MILDER FLAVOUR THAN MOST COMMERCIAL VARIETIES.

MAKES ABOUT 300 ML/ 10 FL OZ

- 2 large egg yolks
- 2 tsp Dijon mustard
- 3/4 tsp salt, or to taste
- 2 tbsp lemon juice or white wine vinegar, plus extra if needed
- about 300 ml/10 fl oz sunflower oil
- white pepper

1. Whizz the egg yolks with the Dijon mustard, salt and white pepper to taste in a food processor, blender or by hand. Add the lemon juice and whizz again.

2. With the motor still running, add the oil, drop by drop at first. When the sauce begins to thicken, the oil can then be added in a slow, steady stream. Taste and adjust the seasoning with extra salt, pepper and lemon juice if necessary. If the sauce seems too thick, slowly add 1 tablespoon of hot water or lemon juice.

3. Use at once or store in a sterilized and airtight container in the refrigerator for up to 1 week.

A GREAT TIP FOR MAKING MAYONNAISE IS TO REMOVE THE EGGS FROM THE REFRIGERATOR IN ORDER TO BRING THEM BACK TO ROOM TEMPERATURE BEFORE USING. THIS WILL ENSURE THE MIXTURE DOESN'T SPLIT.

SWEETCORN RELISH (SWEETCORN CHOW CHOW)

PREP TIME: *20 minutes, plus cooling* **COOK TIME:** *20 minutes*

THIS RELISH MAKES THE PLAINEST BURGER A TREAT, AND IS ESPECIALLY DELICIOUS ON PRAWN & CHIVE BURGERS (SEE PAGE 150).

MAKES 950 G/ 2 LB 2 OZ

3 corn cobs
1 red pepper
1 jalapeño chilli
125 ml/4 fl oz cider vinegar
100 g/3½ oz soft light brown sugar
1 tbsp salt
1 tbsp ground mustard seeds
½ tsp celery seeds
1 red onion, diced

1. Cut the kernels off the corn cobs. Deseed and dice the red pepper and the chilli.

2. Put the corn, red pepper, chilli, vinegar, sugar, salt, mustard seeds and celery seeds into a large saucepan over a medium-high heat and bring to the boil. Reduce the heat to simmering and cook, stirring occasionally, for about 15 minutes until the mixture reduces slightly. The sugar will melt, producing enough liquid to cover the vegetables.

3. Stir the onions into the corn mixture, remove from the heat and ladle the relish into sterilized jars. Seal with lids and leave to cool to room temperature.

STEP 1

STEP 2

THIS TASTY RELISH, LACED WITH MUSTARD SEEDS WILL KEEP FOR UP TO *1* MONTH IN THE REFRIGERATOR.

191

AÏOLI

PREP TIME: *10 minutes, plus chilling*

COOK TIME: *no cooking*

THIS IS A FAMOUS FRENCH GARLIC MAYONNAISE FROM PROVENÇE — DEFINITELY ONE FOR GARLIC LOVERS!

SERVES 4

3 large garlic cloves, finely chopped

2 egg yolks

225 ml/8 fl oz extra virgin olive oil

1 tbsp lemon juice

1 tbsp lime juice

1 tbsp Dijon mustard

1 tbsp chopped fresh tarragon

salt and pepper

fresh tarragon sprig, to garnish

1. Ensure that all the ingredients are at room temperature. Place the garlic and egg yolks in a food processor and process until well blended. With the motor running, pour in the oil teaspoon by teaspoon through the feeder tube until the mixture starts to thicken, then pour in the remaining oil in a thin stream until a thick mayonnaise forms.

2. Add the lemon juice, lime juice, mustard and tarragon and season to taste with salt and pepper. Blend until smooth, then transfer to a non-metallic bowl. Garnish with a tarragon sprig.

3. Cover with clingfilm and refrigerate until required.

GARLIC'S TRADITIONAL USE AS A MEDICINAL PLANT IS DUE TO ITS VARIOUS SULPHUR COMPOUNDS, WHICH WORK TO DETOXIFY, CLEANSE AND REPAIR CELLS TO HELP YOU LOOK AND FEEL YOUNG.

BEEF CHILLI

THIS THICK, DELICIOUS CHILLI IS MADE TO GO ON
TOP OF CHILLI BURGERS (SEE PAGE 36),
OR IT CAN BE SERVED ON ITS OWN.

MAKES 700–850 ML/1¼–1½ PINTS

2 tbsp olive oil

1 onion, chopped

1 red pepper, diced

3 garlic cloves, finely chopped

450 g/1 lb fresh beef mince

2 tbsp chilli powder

½ tsp cayenne pepper

400 g/14 oz canned chopped tomatoes

400 ml/14 fl oz water

2 tbsp chopped fresh parsley

salt and pepper

1. Heat 1 tablespoon of the oil in a large, heavy-based saucepan over a medium heat. Add the onion, red pepper and garlic and sauté for about 5 minutes, stirring, until tender. Remove the sautéed vegetables from the pan, then add the remaining oil.

2. When hot, add the mince with the chilli powder, cayenne pepper, and salt and pepper to taste. Stir to coat the meat with the spices and sauté for about 10 minutes, stirring frequently and breaking up the meat with a wooden spoon, until brown.

3. Add the sautéed vegetables, the tomatoes with their can juices and the water to the pan. Bring to the boil, reduce the heat and simmer for about 45 minutes, stirring occasionally, until the sauce is very thick. Season to taste with salt and pepper and stir in the parsley.

4. Serve immediately or leave to cool, cover with clingfilm and refrigerate for up to 4 days before using.

STEP 1

STEP 3

STEP 3

FOR A BIT OF ADDED INDULGENCE, TOP THE BEEF CHILLI WITH SOME GRATED CHEDDAR CHEESE – DELICIOUS!

QUICK PICKLED ONIONS

PREP TIME: *15 minutes, plus chilling*

COOK TIME: *no cooking*

These sweet, spicy and tangy onions require no heating, so they're easy to make anytime. Include them at the table with all your standard burger condiments.

MAKES ABOUT 450 ML/ 16 FL OZ

225 ml/8 fl oz distilled white vinegar

100 g/3½ oz sugar

1 tsp chipotle powder, or to taste

2 medium red onions, cut into rings

salt

1. In a medium bowl, combine the vinegar, sugar, chipotle powder, and salt to taste. Whisk to dissolve the sugar.

2. Place the onions in a heavy-duty, zip-top bag and pour the marinade over the onions. Toss to coat. Cover and refrigerate for 30 minutes, moving the mixture around a couple of times to evenly distribute the marinade. Drain before serving.

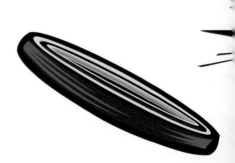

THE ONION IS A TOP HEALTH FOOD, CONTAINING SULPHUR COMPOUNDS THAT ARE NATURAL ANTIBIOTICS OFFERING PROTECTION FROM CANCERS AND HEART DISEASE.

PICKLED JALAPEÑOS

PREP TIME: *15 minutes, plus cooling*

COOK TIME: *15 minutes*

THESE JALAPEÑOS ARE A SIMPLE VERSION OF ESCABECHE, PERFECT FOR GIVING BURGERS A LITTLE EXTRA KICK.

MAKES 950 G/ 2 LB 2 OZ

450 g/1 lb jalapeño chillies
1 white onion
8 garlic cloves
700 ml/1¼ pints cider vinegar or white distilled vinegar
2 tbsp salt
2 bay leaves
2 tsp sugar

1. Remove the stems from the jalapeños and cut the chillies into thick rings.

2. Peel and roughly chop the onion. Peel the garlic cloves.

3. Bring the vinegar, salt, bay leaves and sugar to the boil in a large saucepan. Add the chillies, onions and garlic. Reduce the heat to simmering and cook for about 5 minutes until the chillies are tender.

4. Ladle the chillies, onions and garlic into sterilized jars. Top with enough of the vinegar to cover, then seal with lids. Leave to cool to room temperature then keep in the refrigerator for up to 2 months.

SALMON BURGERS (PAGE 84) WORK PARTICULARLY WELL WITH THESE JALAPEÑOS AS A FIERY TOPPING.

BURGER BUNS

PREP TIME: 20 minutes, plus resting   **COOK TIME:** 15-20 minutes

MAKES 8 BUNS

450 g/1 lb strong white bread flour, plus extra for dusting

1½ tsp salt

2 tsp caster sugar

1 tsp easy-blend dried yeast

150 ml/5 fl oz lukewarm water

150 ml/5 fl oz lukewarm milk

vegetable oil, for brushing

2-3 tbsp sesame seeds

1. Sift the flour and salt together into a bowl and stir in the sugar and yeast. Make a well in the centre and pour in the lukewarm water and milk. Stir well with a wooden spoon until the dough begins to come together, then knead with your hands until it leaves the side of the bowl. Turn out on to a lightly floured surface and knead well for about 10 minutes, until smooth and elastic.

2. Brush a bowl with oil. Shape the dough into a ball, put it in the bowl and put the bowl into a plastic bag or cover with a damp tea towel. Leave to rise in a warm place for 1 hour, until the dough has doubled in volume.

3. Brush two baking sheets with oil. Turn out the dough on to a lightly floured surface and knock back with your fist. Divide it into eight equal-sized pieces, shape each into a ball and put them on the prepared baking sheets. Flatten slightly with a lightly floured hand and put the baking sheets into plastic bags or cover with damp tea towels. Leave to rise in a warm place for 30 minutes.

4. Preheat the oven to 200°C/400°F/Gas Mark 6. Lightly press the centre of each bun with your fingers to release any large air bubbles. Brush the tops with the oil and sprinkle with sesame seeds. Bake for 15-20 minutes, until light golden brown. Transfer to wire racks to cool.

CARAMELIZED ONIONS

PREP TIME: 5 minutes   **COOK TIME: 25 minutes**

SLICED ONIONS, COOKED SLOWLY UNTIL GOLDEN BROWN
AND SLIGHTLY SWEET, ARE A DELICIOUS ACCOMPANIMENT
TO ALL KINDS OF BURGERS.

SERVES 4—6

1-2 tbsp vegetable oil or
olive oil

½ red onion, sliced

½ tsp finely chopped
fresh rosemary, thyme
or oregano (optional)

½ tsp red wine vinegar

salt and pepper

1. Heat enough oil to coat the base of a large frying pan over a medium heat until shimmering. Add the onion and cook on one side for 3 minutes until brown. Add the herbs, if using, stir and continue cooking, stirring occasionally, for about 12 minutes until nicely browned.

2. Season to taste with salt and pepper. Add the vinegar and cook for a further 8-10 minutes until very soft.

3. Serve immediately or leave to cool and store in the refrigerator for up to 3 days.

STEP 1

STEP 2

CARAMELIZED ONIONS ARE BOTH RICH AND SWEET. THEY REQUIRE VERY LITTLE ATTENTION AND ARE EASY TO COOK, MAKING THEM THE PERFECT BURGER TOPPING.

CRISPY ONION RINGS

PREP TIME: *15 minutes*   **COOK TIME:** *15 minutes*

SERVES 4–6

115 g/4 oz plain flour
pinch of salt
1 egg
150 ml/5 fl oz
semi-skimmed milk
4 large onions
vegetable oil, for
deep-frying
chilli powder, to taste
(optional)
salt and pepper
lettuce leaves, to serve

1. To make the batter, sift the flour and a pinch of salt into a large bowl and make a well in the centre. Break the egg into the well and gently beat with a whisk. Gradually whisk in the milk, drawing the flour from the side into the liquid in the centre to form a smooth batter.

2. Leaving the onions whole, slice widthways into 5-mm/¼-inch slices, then separate each slice into rings.

3. Heat the oil in a deep-fat fryer or deep, heavy-based saucepan to 180–190°C/350–375°F, or until a cube of bread browns in 30 seconds.

4. Using the tines of a fork, pick up several onions rings at a time and dip in the batter. Let any excess batter drip off, then add the onions to the oil and deep-fry for 1–2 minutes until they rise to the surface of the oil and become crisp and golden brown. Remove from the oil, drain on kitchen paper and keep warm while deep-frying the remaining onion rings in batches. Do not try to deep-fry too many at a time, as this will reduce the temperature of the oil and the onion rings will absorb some of the oil and become soggy.

5. Season the onion rings with chilli powder, if wished, and salt and pepper to taste, then serve immediately on a bed of lettuce leaves.

THERE ARE DOZENS OF DIFFERENT METHODS THAT PEOPLE CLAIM CAN HELP TO PREVENT YOU FROM CRYING WHILE CUTTING ONIONS, SUCH AS LEAVING THE ROOT INTACT UNTIL THE VERY END, PEELING THEM UNDER RUNNING WATER, CHILLING THEM BEFORE CUTTING, AND EVEN WHISTLING WHILE YOU WORK!

CHIPS

SERVES 4

675 g/1 lb 8 oz large potatoes

sunflower, corn or groundnut oil, for deep-frying

salt and pepper

1. Peel the potatoes and cut into 8-mm/³/₈-inch even-sized fingers. As soon as they are prepared, put them into a large bowl of cold water to prevent discoloration, then leave them to soak for 30 minutes to remove the excess starch.

2. Drain the potatoes and dry well on a clean tea towel. Heat the oil in a deep-fat fryer or large, heavy-based saucepan to 190°C/375°F. If you do not have a thermometer, test the temperature by dropping a potato finger into the oil. If it sinks, the oil isn't hot enough; if it floats and the oil bubbles around the potato, it is ready. Carefully add a small batch of potatoes to the oil (this is to ensure even cooking and to avoid reducing the temperature of the oil) and deep-fry for 5–6 minutes until soft but not browned. Remove from the oil and drain well on kitchen paper. Leave to cool for at least 5 minutes. Continue to deep-fry the remaining potatoes in the same way, allowing the oil to return to the correct temperature each time.

3. When ready to serve, reheat the oil to 200°C/400°F. Add the potatoes, in small batches and deep-fry for 2–3 minutes until golden brown. Remove from the oil and drain on kitchen paper. Serve immediately, seasoned to taste with salt and pepper.

French fries, pommes frites or chips, from chunky to shoestring – call them what you wish, but any burger – from the most simple to gourmet, wouldn't be the same without this classic accompaniment.

CREAMY POTATO SALAD

PREP TIME: *30 minutes, plus chilling*   **COOK TIME:** *30 minutes*

COOL AND CREAMY, THIS SALAD SHOULD BE AN INTEGRAL PART OF ANY BARBECUE.

SERVES 8

1.25 kg/2 lb 12 oz waxy potatoes

125 ml/4 fl oz mayonnaise

50 ml/2 fl oz soured cream

90 ml/3 fl oz white wine vinegar

1 tsp wholegrain mustard

½ tsp dried dill

75 g/2¾ oz red onions, finely chopped

30 g/1 oz celery, finely chopped

¼ cup chopped gherkins

40 g/1½ oz roasted red peppers, chopped

2 hard-boiled eggs, chopped (optional)

salt and pepper

1. Place the unpeeled potatoes in a medium-sized saucepan and cover with water by a few inches. Add salt, bring to the boil over a high heat, then reduce the heat and simmer for 20–30 minutes until fork-tender.

2. Put the mayonnaise, soured cream, vinegar, mustard, dill, and salt and pepper to taste into a bowl and mix together.

3. Drain the potatoes and leave to cool slightly, then slip off the skins with your fingers or with a paring knife. Chop the potatoes into 1-cm/½-inch pieces and add to the dressing while still warm. Stir in the onion, celery, gherkins, peppers and egg, if using. Cover and chill for at least 2 hours or overnight.

MACARONI SALAD

PREP TIME: *30 minutes, plus chilling* **COOK TIME:** *10 minutes*

THIS CLASSIC SALAD IS AN ESSENTIAL PART OF PICNICS AND GOES WELL WITH A JUICY BURGER.

SERVES 6–8

225 g/8 oz dried elbow macaroni

50 ml/2 fl oz mayonnaise, plus extra if needed

50 ml/2 fl oz natural yogurt

1 tbsp fresh lemon juice

½ tsp garlic salt

½ tsp pepper

40 g/1½ oz celery, diced

40 g/1½ oz spring onions, finely chopped

40 g/1½ oz black olives, finely chopped

50 g/1¾ oz tomatoes, finely chopped

2 tbsp chopped fresh flat-leaf parsley

salt and pepper

1. Bring a medium-sized saucepan of lightly salted water to the boil, add the macaroni and cook according to the packet instructions. Drain.

2. Meanwhile, combine the mayonnaise, yogurt, lemon juice, garlic salt and the pepper in a large bowl. Stir in the hot macaroni, then add the celery, spring onions, olives, tomatoes and parsley. Season to taste with salt and pepper and add more mayonnaise if it seems dry, then leave to cool completely.

3. Cover with clingfilm and chill for at least 2 hours until cold. Serve cold. The salad will keep in the refrigerator for up to 3 days.

ONE OF THE MOST POPULAR ADD-ONS TO THIS AMERICAN BBQ STAPLE IS HARD-BOILED EGGS. SIMPLY HARD-BOIL THREE EGGS AND CHOP BEFORE ADDING TO THE BOWL WITH THE REST OF THE INGREDIENTS.

FRESH LEMONADE

PREP TIME: *15 minutes, plus standing*   **COOK TIME:** *no cooking*

THERE IS NOTHING MORE REFRESHING ON A HOT SUMMER'S DAY THAN A GLASS OR TWO OF HOME-MADE LEMONADE – THERE IS, OF COURSE, THE ADDED BONUS THAT THERE ARE NO ARTIFICIAL ADDITIVES.

SERVES 6

4 large lemons, preferably unwaxed
175 g/6 oz caster sugar
850 ml/1½ pints boiling water
ice cubes

1. Scrub the lemons well, then dry. Using a vegetable peeler, peel three of the lemons very thinly. Place the peel in a large jug or basin, add the sugar and boiling water and stir well until the sugar has dissolved. Cover the jug and leave to stand for at least 3 hours, stirring occasionally. Meanwhile, squeeze the juice from the 3 lemons and reserve.

2. Remove and discard the lemon peel and stir in the reserved lemon juice. Thinly slice the remaining lemon and cut the slices in half. Add to the lemonade together with the ice cubes. Stir and serve immediately.

You can try using oranges or limes or a mixture of all three fruits for some equally refreshing thirst-quenchers.

ORANGE & LIME ICED TEA

PREP TIME: 10 minutes, plus chilling

COOK TIME: less than 5 minutes

ICED TEA IS ALWAYS REFRESHING AND EVEN IF YOU ARE NOT A TEA DRINKER, THIS VERSION IS ESPECIALLY FRESH AND FRUITY. KEEP SOME IN THE REFRIGERATOR IF YOU DON'T USE IT ALL UP.

SERVES 2

300 ml/10 fl oz water
2 tea bags
100 ml/3½ fl oz orange juice
4 tbsp lime juice
1–2 tbsp brown sugar
ice cubes

TO DECORATE

lime wedge
granulated sugar
orange or lime slices

1. Pour the water into a saucepan and bring to the boil. Remove from the heat, add the tea bags and leave to infuse for 5 minutes. Remove the tea bags and leave the tea to cool to room temperature. Transfer to a jug, cover with clingfilm and chill in the refrigerator for at least 45 minutes.

2. When the tea has chilled, pour in the orange juice and lime juice. Add sugar to taste.

3. Take two glasses and rub the rims with a lime wedge, then dip them in granulated sugar to frost. Put the ice cubes into the glasses and pour over the tea. Decorate with orange or lime slices and serve immediately.

KA-POW!

FROM SOFT DRINKS AND BEER TO BLENDED DRINKS, ALWAYS OFFER A GOOD CHOICE AT SUMMER PARTIES. INCLUDE PLENTY OF BOTTLED WATER ON YOUR SHOPPING LIST, AND PLACE BUCKETS FILLED WITH ICE CUBES AT VARIOUS POINTS SO GUESTS CAN HELP THEMSELVES.

CLUB MOJITO

PREP TIME: 5 minutes   **COOK TIME:** no cooking

THIS TRADITIONAL CUBAN COCKTAIL HAS RECENTLY COME BACK INTO VOGUE. IMPRESS YOUR GUESTS WITH THIS REFRESHING, REVITALIZING AND DELICIOUS TREAT!

SERVES 1

1 tsp syrup de gomme
a few fresh mint leaves
juice of ½ lime
ice cubes
2 measures Jamaican rum
soda water
dash of Angostura bitters

1. Put the syrup, mint leaves and lime juice in a glass and crush or muddle the mint leaves.

2. Add ice and the rum, then top up with soda water to taste. Finish with a dash of Angostura bitters. Serve immediately.

216

217

MARGARITA

PREP TIME: 5 minutes **COOK TIME:** no cooking

THIS COCKTAIL, INVENTED IN 1942 IN MEXICO, IS A MORE CIVILIZED VERSION OF THE ORIGINAL WAY TO DRINK TEQUILA – A LICK OF SALT FROM THE BACK OF THE HAND, A SHOT OF TEQUILA AND A SUCK OF LIME JUICE!

SERVES 1

- lime wedges
- coarse salt
- 3 measures white tequila
- 1 measure Triple Sec or Cointreau
- 2 measures lime juice
- cracked ice cubes

1. Rub the rim of a chilled cocktail glass with a lime wedge and then dip in a saucer of coarse salt to frost.

2. Shake the tequila, Triple Sec and lime juice vigorously over cracked ice until well frosted.

3. Strain into the glass and dress with a lime wedge. Serve immediately.

THIS REFRESHING PICK-ME-UP OFFERS A CLASSIC COMBINATION OF INGREDIENTS THAT MAKE IT UNSURPRISING THAT IT'S ONE OF THE WORLD'S MOST POPULAR COCKTAILS.

223